DESIGNING WITH

TREES

DESIGNING WITH

TREES

The complete guide to using trees in your garden

ANTHONY PAUL
&
YVONNE REES

Foreword by Arthur Hellyer

WINDWARD

for Winnie

DESIGNING WITH TREES

DESIGNING WITH TREES
was conceived and produced by
Anthony Paul, Susan Berry and Steven Wooster
for Duane Paul Design Team, Unit 30,
Ransome's Dock, Parkgate Road, London SW11 4NP

WINDWARD
An imprint owned by W H Smith and Son Limited
Registered No 237811, England
Trading as WHS Distributors, St. John's House,
East Street, Leicester LE1 6NE

ISBN 0 7112 0499 3

Originated by Universal Colour Scanning, Hong Kong
Typeset by Chambers Wallace, London
Printed and bound in Hong Kong by Kwong Fat

Editor Susan Berry
Assistant editor Susan George

Editorial consultants David Carr & Leo Pemberton

Design by Steven Wooster

Picture research The Garden Picture Library

CONTENTS

Foreword

Everyone agrees that trees are the most conspicuous living objects in countryside and garden, and yet trees are often poorly placed and ill chosen. Even in great landscape gardens I see trees that are well grown and very beautiful in themselves but which nevertheless impede rather than enhance the intended picture.

Much of this is due to a failure to visualize at the outset what the trees will look like when they reach maturity. Most trees take at least fifteen years to make a significant effect, twenty years to impart an air of permanence and at least another twenty to reach maturity. Most will continue to live far longer than that and some of the most admired trees in man-made landscapes were planted at least a century ago. It is very difficult to think that far ahead, to visualize the eventual shape, height and spread of every sapling and to plant accordingly.

If at the outset trees are given all the space they will eventually require they will inevitably look sparse in the early years. The sensible thing is to plant more thickly for quick effect but with the clear intention to thin progressively as they grow. This also requires great imagination for it is all too easy to discover, as culling times arrive, that some of the better varieties, intended to be permanent, have to go while others, that were to be temporary, must be retained in order to preserve a correct balance.

Designing With Trees will help tree planters to avoid these faults and get things right from the outset. Anthony Paul is a landscape architect who takes special delight in designs that look natural though they have involved very careful thought. He and his co-author, Yvonne Rees, offer advice that is clear and to the point and the pictures selected are a dream. Readers who study both with care should be able to reduce their mistake rate to near zero but if things do not work out exactly to plan it is better to change at once than to let things drag on as they are, hoping that they may become better. Trees are too important to be allowed to become a nuisance.

Arthur Hellyer

Introduction

We tend to take the trees in our gardens, streets and parks for granted. Indeed, it is difficult to visualize an urban setting without its trees – the only image that springs to mind is the bleakness of a new housing estate before the landscapers move in. But it took a freak gale which ripped through southern England in 1987, devastating thousands upon thousands of trees overnight, to shock us into an awareness of how much trees contribute to the variety and beauty of the landscape.

After the utilitarianism of the post-war years, town planners of the world's major towns and cities at last began to realize the visual and psychological benefits of including trees in their schemes. Green belts of tree planting with small parks and plantations linked to existing woodlands are now a prerequisite of much new town development, and the landscapers now work closely with the architects from the very first planning decisions.

The monotonous spread of concrete and glass in cities can have a dehumanizing effect. To counteract this, and to breathe life into dusty streets, the city of Tokyo has provided green corridors of trees to separate pedestrians from the closely packed buildings. In just a few years, thanks to the extensive planting of *Ginkgo biloba*, the ancient Maidenhair Tree whose leaf is the symbol of the city, there has been a remarkable transformation. Ginkgo grows quickly and is extremely pollution resistant; as a result the planting has achieved a 98 per cent establishment rate.

But the advantage of trees in town and city gardens is more than just aesthetic. Trees do a wonderful clean-up job, absorbing acid rain and other pollutants in the air – one of the reasons why pollution-resistant species like the Italian Alder (*Alnus cordata*), limes and liriodendrons are so frequently chosen as street trees. In the long term, in country areas, trees also provide us with valuable humus-rich soil from their dead leaves, and by acting as a windbreak and by the binding action of the roots, help to preserve valuable topsoil and slow down the rate of erosion.

RIGHT *Where a long view of the garden is in danger of disappearing into the distance, grouping trees of different heights and foliage patterns will add depth and provide an interesting backdrop, particularly at the end of the year when deciduous types begin to change colour. Note how shorter, denser, more decorative trees like* Sorbus *in front of the tall trunks and the 'net-curtain' foliage of a line of beech in the background have created a three dimensional effect right down to the much smaller contrasts of formal clipped* Ligustrum *and fiery-foliaged* Cotinus coggygria *'Royal Purple' in the foreground.*

Trees in your garden

Because trees are the largest living vertical elements in the garden, it makes sense for them to

be the starting point in any new garden plan. Some of the larger shrubs perform the same role and we have, in this book, included both trees (normally defined as having a single woody stem and branches that persist all year round) and arboreal shrubs – in other words shrubs with a tree-like habit or that are large enough to perform the role of a tree.

Most of us are familiar with a dismally small number of trees, but there is, in fact, a wonderful variety of shapes, sizes and forms of tree to choose from, and once you know of their existence it can be difficult to decide between them. Although it is tempting to pick the ones that take your fancy in pictures or as saplings in a nursery, to get the full benefit from a tree you need to think much more carefully about its attributes in terms of design and its positioning in the garden, as well as its practical use.

The range of trees suitable for planting in gardens is growing all the time, as new hybrids and cultivars come on the scene, sometimes specially bred to give bigger, better fruits, brighter foliage or more seasons of interest. In this book we have listed a large number of the species and cultivars available, but there are, of course, many, many more and it will pay you to contact some of the specialist tree nurseries and browse through their catalogues.

Although the new hybrids and cultivars have much to offer, do not desert the old-established species completely. They have their place, too, particularly in country gardens where they blend much more naturally with any indigenous trees in the surrounding landscape. Like everything else, trees go in and out of fashion and it pays not to follow it too slavishly. Just because everyone in your street has a particular magnolia (probably because the local garden centre stocks it prominently) you do not have to follow suit.

The visual effects

Tree shapes can vary considerably from the cone-shaped firs and columnar pines to large round-headed beeches and maples and to the generous wide-spreading forms of *Albizia* and crab apple (*Malus*). There are tall narrow trees like poplars and trailing pendulous ones like the weeping willow. You can pick a particular shape to suit a specific location or you can group together trees with different shapes to make a group with an interestingly varied outline. Small trees with an attractive spreading habit make good subjects for a single focal point in a small garden, particularly when they have the added bonus of attractive flowers, foliage and fruit at different seasons, like the crab apples and some of the hawthorn family. Narrow cone-shaped and columnar trees such as firs and pines make good subjects for planting in pairs to frame a gateway, or a view.

Where space is limited, or where you wish to create a deliberately formal atmosphere, you can clip or train trees into more artificial shapes – cordon and espalier fruit trees can be trained against walls in small gardens, and slow-growing

Some distinctive forms of conifer foliage

trees like yew and bay can be clipped to form handsome geometric shapes in a formal garden.

The foliage of the tree plays a major role in any garden in its shape, from the hand-shaped leaves of the maple to the rowan's feathery fern-like ones, in its texture – furry, glossy, deeply-veined or crinkle-edged – and above all in its colour, from the light silvery grey of *Sorbus aria* to the rich gold of *Robinia pseudacacia* 'Frisia' and the deep reddish-purple of some of the Japanese maples. Many trees provide you with a changing spectacle of massed arrays of colour – fresh spring leaves, glorious flowers and then, when the rest of the garden is dying back in autumn, a wonderful burst of foliage tints in reds, golds, copper and bronze. Many trees have attractive fruit as a bonus, ranging from the bright, purely ornamental scarlet berries of the holly to the delicious edible fruit of the crab apple or almond.

In winter the framework of the garden is most noticeable, and it is here that trees have a major role to play. The deciduous trees offer striking outlines of bare branches while the evergreens – a holly, an evergreen oak (*Quercus ilex*) or a pine – fill out the garden with some winter substance. In winter, too, the virtues of attractive bark – the highly polished bark of the ornamental cherry, the deep furrows of *Robinia pseudacacia* and the attractive peeling tatters of *Acer griseum* – are seen at their best in the garden.

Your choice of trees can

Different leaf shapes of some of the broad-leaved trees

influence the style or atmosphere of the garden: pines can give it an alpine feel, Japanese maples blend well with the stone and sand of typical oriental gardens and silvery-grey small-leaved trees can give it a Mediterranean appearance.

Practical considerations

Precisely because trees are larger than the other plants in your garden, their eventual size and their speed of growth need to be considered carefully. Some trees have been specially bred as small specimens (including many of the Japanese maples) while others grow so slowly that although they will make 21·5 or 24·5 m (70 or 80 ft) by the time they are fully grown, it will take almost a lifetime for them to achieve it. Some will grow more quickly or slowly depending on the conditions – making 30 m (100 ft) eventually in an environment that is congenial but only half that in a more hostile situation.

Growing trees in tubs or containers will restrict their growth and can be used to advantage to keep some trees within reasonable proportions for a small garden or patio.

Where you are looking to trees to provide screening or shelter, you obviously need to pick the faster-growing forms, which are ideal for the boundary of a country garden. But if you want to plant trees in a hedge for an eventual height of 2 m (6 ft) or so, beware of ones that are going to be difficult to control after they have reached the desired height. You would be better off providing temporary screening while a slower-growing, more dwarf shrub grows to the height you want.

To get the best from your trees, their needs in terms of soil, climate and aspect must be met. While some, like rowans, hawthorns and birches, are salt- and pollution-resistant, making them ideal subjects for inner city or coastal gardens, others will fail to thrive in those conditions. Fast-growing shallow-rooted trees like willow may be useful for a quick effect but they should be sited with care as their roots can interfere with other plants, and the deeper-rooted specimens like poplar can damage drainpipes if planted too close to them. Some trees do best in very damp conditions – the willows, birches, alders and sweet gum. Others, like hornbeam, prefer dry soil. Most of the flowering trees like a sunny situation although there are a few smaller trees and arboreal shrubs, like *Camellia japonica* and *Rhododendron arborea* that will tolerate light shade.

As well as providing invaluable vertical interest, trees can serve a variety of roles in the garden. One of the most important is for screening – either for privacy or for protection from noise, pollution or from prevailing winds. One or two trees are often sufficient to block an unattractive view or screen you from neighbours; beware, though, of the bigger trees like sycamores or the Norway Maple which not only mask the eyesore effectively but block out almost all the available light as well. The foliage of birches, for example, is lighter and more attractive but does the job of screening just as effectively.

Trees for shade need equally careful planning. Often the shade is only required in summer, so deciduous trees make the best choice, and preferably those with a light, dappled canopy rather than a dense spread of heavy foliage. Rowans and catalpas offer fresh, light foliage that is ideal for screening patios and seating areas.

One of the reasons why some keen gardeners are reluctant to plant trees is because they cast shade, and take up space that the gardener is keen to devote to other plants. But there is no need for the soil under the tree to be barren. If the trees are well chosen, casting only light shade, not only can a number of plants be grown under their canopies, but the light shade and shelter can also be used to advantage to grow some of the more unusual shade-loving woodland plants, and certainly a host of spring bulbs which all flower before the tree bursts into leaf in late spring. In a large garden, a copse of trees that casts quite heavy shade can be a useful low-maintenance asset, as weeds will be reluctant to germinate.

Plotting the design

Having established the dimensions of your garden, it is a good idea to draw out a plan of it to scale on graph paper, marking the trees in as a rough circular outline in proportion with the expected eventual spread of the branches – this not only gives you a good idea of how far the roots will spread (they rarely exceed the spread

Trees for a small town garden
*A small town garden no more than 6 × 9 m (20 × 30 ft) has enough space for a good selection of trees and shrubs. In this oriental-style garden the trees have been chosen to provide a succession of interest from flower colour in shades of white and pink and good foliage colour. The rowan (*Sorbus*) and the crab apple (*Malus*) will also provide edible fruits in the autumn, while the maple (*Acer*) leaves will turn rich shades of gold and bronze. The trees have been underplanted with shade-loving ground covering plants, like hostas, pulmonarias with attractively variegated leaves,* Pachysandra terminalis *and ferns. Pots of annuals on the deck make an additional splash of colour in summer. Climbers like the clematis are useful for threading colour over trees or walls and, for all seasons interest, variegated ivies could be grown over the fences. On a practical level the garden requires only minimal maintenance, a decided plus for busy city dwellers; it also makes an excellent habitat for birds and squirrels who will take advantage of the autumn fruits if you do not do so first.*

Malus tschonoskii
Prunus 'Pandora'
Acer japonicum
Sorbus aria 'Mitchellii'
Clematis montana 'Rubra'
Camellia japonica
Shade-loving ferns
Mixed planting of Pulmonaria sp.
Impatiens sp.
Miscanthus sinensis

of the branches) but will also indicate any areas of shade where you may have to consider the underplanting carefully.

Try to aim for a mixture of evergreen and deciduous trees to give year-round interest to the garden, and include one or two trees that have something of value to offer at all seasons.

When deciding where to site the trees, pay attention to the naturally shady and sunny sides of the garden, so that the trees afford shade only where it is most needed. Make sure that they do not encroach too much on the house, or overhang patios, paving or pools where dropping leaves and fruit could be a problem.

In small urban gardens you will have to take account of buildings and garden walls, and make sure that the trees are not planted so close that they form a nuisance. How close you can plant a tree really depends on its type. Although there used to be a rule that you should plant a tree no closer to a building than its eventual height, this is very rarely adhered to these days. Much more important is the speed of growth, the form of the roots and the shape of the tree, and the density of the canopy. Get advice from the garden centre or nursery when you buy the tree.

With luck you will already have some trees in your garden, but you do perhaps need to consider how best to supplement them and whether they are all earning their keep. It pays to keep a tree wherever possible, but if it is threatening to completely overshadow the garden or damage the buildings, then it would be best to have it removed professionally rather than lop its limbs so drastically that it becomes an eyesore.

On a purely practical level, it pays to plant your trees with great care. They are not cheap to buy and it is important that they flourish and grow well. A miserable, ill-prepared planting hole will result, at the least, in a tree that fails to establish itself properly for several years.

Precisely because trees, in the main, are imposing plants and long-lived ones, they will last in your garden scheme long after the other plants have perished or been removed by future owners. They deserve special consideration because you are planting them, in all likelihood, not just for your own enjoyment but also for posterity.

Trees for a country garden
*In a medium-sized country garden you will probably have enough space to create a mini-woodland garden with a dozen different species of tree. If they are chosen with care, they will provide an endless variety of leaf colour and shape, flowers and berries. In this garden they have been underplanted with grass that is left unmown until late summer so that spring bulbs can naturalize, followed later by wildflowers, while the lawn surrounding the patio area is kept neatly trimmed. A clipped evergreen hedge of yew (*Taxus baccata*) shelters the patio on one side, while a specimen tree (*Malus *'Red Jade'), with its neat form, glossy leaves, spring blossom and colourful crab apples in autumn, provides year-round interest nearby. Pots of ferns and annuals can be used to add interest to the patio at different seasons.*

Keeping the tree planting largely to the perimeter of the garden gives it an open spacious feeling, as well as providing both a useful windbreak and welcome privacy.

Betula papyrifera
Acer rubrum
Acer saccharum
Malus 'Red Jade'
Catalpa bignonioides
Hostas
Taxus baccata

—I—

GARDEN THEMES

In ancient woodlands, trees seeded themselves and the fittest and best adapted to the conditions survived. But when choosing trees for our gardens we have to select them with special care if they are to blend in with the surroundings, and with the garden planting as well as the landscape beyond. Properly chosen, they make a splendid and eye-catching addition to the garden, providing shelter, privacy and shade as well as striking colour, fascinating leaf shapes and, often, attractive flowers, berries or bark. In this chapter we take a look at a variety of garden settings and suggest ways of incorporating trees – singly and in groups – into the garden scheme so that their particular attributes can be shown off to best advantage

The bronze foliage of Acer palmatum *'Atropurpureum' frames the golden-leaved maple,* A.p. *'Aureum'*

Town Gardens

We often forget how important trees are in town and city gardens. They have an essential role to play not just as a screen for noise and to provide privacy, but also as a valuable filter for urban pollution. They also bring much needed oxygen to starved town gardens, and provide both sanctuary and sustenance for wildlife. Although in heavily polluted areas it may not be advisable to grow fruit trees for your own consumption, at least one small tree with berries, like the Cockspur Thorn (*Crataegus crus-galli*) with its bright red haws, that attracts birds and a tree with flowers that attract butterflies and bees, like the purple-flowered *Buddleia davidii*, would be well worth including in the garden.

Coping with pollution

Successful street planting provides living proof of certain trees' ability to survive and flourish under conditions where even we begin to wilt. But you may be surprised at the wide variety of choice from the bright green ancient Maidenhair Tree (*Ginkgo biloba*) to the dense-headed Norway Maple (*Acer platanoides*), which will grow both well and quickly. Although these, like the horse chestnuts and American buckeyes (*Aesculus*) and the limes (*Tilia*), are all large trees, there are many other smaller trees that will cope equally well, including *Sorbus, Laburnum, Magnolia* and the cherry plums (*Prunus cerasifera*), as well as the less common Amur Cork Tree (*Phellodendron amurense*) with its dark cracked bark and good yellow autumn colour. You could also grow a smaller form (*Liriodendron chinense*) of the popular Tulip Tree (*L. tulipifera*). *L. chinense* does not flower so freely and its leaves are paler, but otherwise it is very similar.

Where space is limited, and where neighbours are very close, it is important that the trees are not too tall, and that their branches do not encroach on neighbouring property and their roots do not damage drainage systems. Some of the best trees for town gardens are the small ornamental ones like the crabs (*Malus*) and hawthorns (*Crataegus*), as well as the hybrid forms of the spectacular Japanese-bred ornamental cherries that have been specially developed for their compact habit. Since not all nurseries are completely accurate on the

LEFT *A dramatic framework of evergreen planting in the shape of tall columnar* Juniperus chinensis *and ivies clinging to the tall walls sets the scene for this tiny courtyard where dark formal pots of clipped box (* Buxus sempervirens*) and container-grown exotics such as* Cycas revoluta *and camellia encourage an intimate atmosphere. The protected environment of the town garden will often provide an ideal opportunity to grow more tender species.*

ABOVE *The delicate fresh green foliage and slender black and white stems of the Birch require a neutral background to emphasize its fine features. The stark green and white theme of this backyard corner was inspired by two groups of* Betula pendula, *framing an elegant bay window and highlighted against a white painted wall. White gravel ground cover serves to emphasize the ghostly pale trunks, with a small trough of clipped, dark green box grown as a small hedge, as relief.*

eventual size of some of the trees on offer, it does pay to check the trees out in a reputable reference book before you buy.

Provided you choose the species with an eye to their eventual height and spread, you could grow at least half a dozen trees in a garden no bigger than 4·5 × 13·5 m (15 × 45 ft). For example, a *Prunus subhirtella*, a *Magnolia stellata*, a Japanese maple (grown in a pot or tub), a *Crataegus*, a *Robinia* and a *Buddleia* would give year-round interest of flowers, foliage tints and berries, provide welcome but not over-dense shade, and still leave plenty of space in full sun for a good selection of herbaceous bedding plants.

Providing shade

Dappled shade is often useful in a town garden where glaring white walls and reflecting glass can make it far too hot to grow an interesting range of plants. The best shade is neither too dense nor too widespread, and some of the arboreal shrubs are a good choice in this situation. The small shrubby *Magnolia stellata* which is smothered in star-shaped blooms in spring is a good choice (ideal for a tiny front garden too). Equally, two forms of *Robinia*, *R. hispida* (the Rose Acacia) and *R. kelseyi* (Kelsey's Acacia) with their cut leaves are good choices for the small garden. The Rose Acacia, as its name implies, has attractive rose-coloured pea-blossom flowers and *R. kelseyi* has similar deep pink flowers, as well as handsome bristly red seed pods. The latter is slightly taller than the Rose Acacia with narrower leaflets.

A patio or seating area may well need to be shaded to the south or west (or north if you live in the southern hemisphere) from the hot afternoon sun; a dense-foliaged tree will create a dank gloomy area, so opt instead for something making attractive dappled shade like the round-headed Yellow Wood (*Cladrastis lutea*) which grows to about 20 m (65 ft). (It also has deep roots so it will not upturn your paving.) One of the pretty rowans (*Sorbus*), another smallish tree with light, attractive, ferny, foliage and excellent autumn colour, would be an equally good choice.

In the larger town garden you might like to consider not just larger or broader trees, but also more ambitious tree planting schemes. A miniature woodland of small trees like the Manna Ash (*Fraxinus ornus*), hawthorn (*Crataegus*), Wild Cherry (*Prunus avium*), dogwoods (*Cornus*), *Sorbus*, and some of the smaller beech trees, will give a taste of the country in the middle of a city. You can underplant with spring bulbs, primroses, anemones and foxgloves.

Year-round appeal

In a small space, trees must work hard for their living so it is important to choose varieties that offer good value most of the year like the Japanese maples; *Acer palmatum* 'Dissectum Atropurpureum' is an excellent example here since it does not grow very large and produces wonderful foliage colour and shape for most of the year. In fact you are almost spoiled for choice with small ornamental trees whose effect might be lost or swamped in a larger, grander setting: Paperbark Maple (*Acer griseum*) with its dark red shoots,

LEFT *One or two of the smaller, decorative trees are often sufficient to screen and shade a small patio. If you choose a pretty deciduous type, you will not lose valuable light in winter. Many have the advantage of sweet-scented spring blossom and edible fruits, like these mature apple trees.*

BELOW *These standard catalpas mark out and partially shade an informal seating area, their mop heads of attractive foliage adding height and dappled shade, with the advantage that their tall naked stems do not block views of the rest of the garden or make the area too enclosed.*

LEFT *A small light-foliaged specimen tree makes an excellent eye-catcher against darker evergreen planting. This fresh-green leaved orange tree (*Citrus*) highlights a bend in the path, against a red-studded pomegranate (*Punica granata*) and a sea of grey* Santolina.

BELOW *When a balcony or roof garden has spectacular views across the tree tops, formal trees grown in tubs and containers provide both a leafy link and interesting contrast. These standard bay trees (*Laurus nobilis*) soften the dark timber framework which in its turn protects and shades the trees from sun and wind.*

ABOVE *Without its dramatically positioned* Picea pungens glauca *'Procumbens' this tiny rear garden would lose all its impact. The dark green climber* Parthenocissus quinquefolia *and the grey spreading* Cedrus atlantica *'Glauca' whose light densely covered branches look permanently weighted with snow, make a permanent framework for a small informal pool, particularly in winter when they are perfectly balanced by dramatic boulders and practical timber decking.*

orange-brown bark, silvery foliage and autumn colour; the Ornamental Crab (*Malus* 'Golden Hornet') which has white spring blossom, a compact upright habit and the most luscious golden fruits; or the small (4 m/12 ft) *Enkianthus campanulatus* with red shoots, multiple branches and late spring flowers which asks only a lime-free soil, sunshine and shelter.

Patios and roof gardens

In a paved patio, small clipped trees will enhance a formal design, and they look particularly good with statuary or raised beds. If you grow them in tubs and containers, you can choose from more tender species as well. Evergreens like bay or box can be clipped into interesting shapes, pom-pom heads, spirals or cones, and are also useful for enclosing and sheltering small patio areas, protecting them from wind and dust.

Roof gardens are becoming increasingly popular in densely populated cities, but they are not easy to plant or maintain successfully. In most cases, the weight of the planting and the pots has to be taken into account, and that probably means that only the very smallest trees can be grown. Roof gardens are, obviously, exposed and many species of trees will not stand up to battering from strong, cold winds, especially when young. You will have to shelter them with screening or limit your choice to species that are wind-resistant, like the upright Pea Tree (*Caragana arborescens*) or the pretty grey Oleaster (*Elaeagnus angustifolia*), which will also cope well with drought and pollution, and still produce lovely silver-grey foliage, fragrant flowers and yellow autumn berries. Many of the conifers will cope with an exposed site, but they will look better if you limit the number of shapes and colours.

COUNTRY & WOODLAND GARDENS

THE BEAUTY of most country gardens is that they are large enough to incorporate a leafy woodland walk, a small spinney or possibly an orchard. A ready-made landscape of trees beyond your boundary can be used to advantage as a focal point or as a backdrop, your tree planting designed to lead the eye towards a spectacular view or arranged to frame a vista. To achieve harmony with the surrounding countryside the majority of the trees you choose should be natural, indigenous species – with only the occasional specimen tree, like a Japanese Maple (*Acer palmatum*) or perhaps a Field Maple (*Acer campestre*), included. The chief attractions of a country garden lie in recreating, on a smaller scale, the shady pleasures of the woodland. You should be aiming for species trees in a massed group that imitates natural juxtapositions of trees.

Trees for country and woodland gardens are the ones we are familiar with from childhood in the heady days when all our senses were more acute – the feel of rough bark, the scent of wet leaves and the taste of autumn fruit. Avoid the showy cultivars with big flowers and opt instead for foliage

RIGHT *The neatly clipped evergreens link the levels created by the sunken pool to the rest of the garden, the clipped domes serving as a counterpoint to the horizontal lines of the dry stone walls and hedges. The three large smoke trees (*Cotinus coggygria*) with their spreading heads and deep crimson foliage bring life and variety to the garden in autumn.*

LEFT *Spring bulbs and woodland flowers fringing a mossy stone path make a delightful woodland walk early in the year before the trees produce their leafy canopy. The strong skeletal shapes of trunks and branches are still attractive and trees have been staggered to avoid any impression of a formal walkway or avenue. This is an effect that could be created in a garden of less than a third of an acre.*

RIGHT *The lovely Japanese maples are a wonderful asset in large gardens as well as small. Here, a beautiful* Acer palmatum *'Atropurpureum' has been used to frame a view across an informal country lake. A simple staggered bridge emphasizes the tree's oriental origins and catches superb reflections, particularly in autumn. A bed of pebbles is all that is needed under the shade of the branches, reinforcing the oriental theme.*

texture and contrast of form. It is worth including one or two for their outstanding foliage shape or colour or unusual form: the unexpected sight of the peeling cinnamon bark of the Paperbark Maple (*Acer griseum*), for example, or the fine texture of a Silver Weeping Pear (*Pyrus salicifolia* 'Pendula'), surrounded by much larger trees.

Creating a natural effect demands just as careful planning as the more formal scheme. Trees will look best planted in groups of uneven numbers, preferably either in arcs or staggered rows; species should be positioned with regard to height, breadth and habit so that they can be seen in their full glory: put smaller trees like *Malus floribunda* (Japanese Crab) at the front of your line of view and larger stately trees, like *Fagus sylvatica*, at the centre back. To maintain interest all year include one or more of the spring-blossoming trees with small single white or pink flowers, like the Wild Cherry (*Prunus avium*) or hawthorn (*Crataegus monogyna*) as well as one or two with good autumn colour, such as rowan (*Sorbus*), beech (*Fagus*) or birch (*Betula*).

Most country gardens are not large enough for a full-scale woodland so you are more likely to want to plant a tiny spinney of fewer than half a dozen trees – say two small oaks (*Quercus*), a birch (*Betula*), a Bronvaux Medlar (+*Crataegomespilus dardarii*) and a rowan (*Sorbus*) – or a leafy walkway between small trees like *Crataegus monogyna*, or perhaps a boundary screen of oaks.

If you do not have room for an orchard of fruit trees, you might consider including one or two of the following: a hazel (*Corylus avellana*), a magnificent walnut (*Juglans regia*), Common Elder (*Sambucus nigra*), one of the edible crab apples (*Malus*) or rowan (*Sorbus*), depending on soil and climate. Pretty enough to be grown as specimen trees, their edible fruits, nuts and berries are a delicious bonus.

If trees play a prominent role, a shady environment will be created and will offer the opportunity to grow interesting woodland plants: drifts of wildflowers in the more open areas and, under the trees, shade-lovers like celandines, bluebells, wild garlic and wood anemones.

RIGHT *Variety of shape and size will give your garden breadth and a feeling of maturity. The much smaller bronze-tinted shrubs among these more substantial oaks (*Quercus robur*) emphasize a curve and their warm colour is echoed by the short shrubby mass of heather (*Erica vagans*) in the foreground which pulls the scheme together and creates a more intimate feel as you approach the house.*

Water Gardens

Trees are natural companions for water features; most trees require a great deal of water, absorbing moisture through their highly efficient root system or their leaves. Some are more thirsty than others and these are the trees found in the wild with their roots in the banks of streams and ponds or actually submerged in the water – the willows, alders and beeches. They make a perfect backdrop for a large informal pool or water feature in the garden, adding height and protection to the general scheme and an ever-changing pattern of reflections.

Unfortunately, there are drawbacks, particularly for small gardens. Water-greedy trees like *Salix* and *Populus* may damage the drainage system and the water supply pipes (should they leak) and too many such trees in the garden, though not likely to affect the natural water table, could rapidly reduce the level of ponds. Trees can also be a nuisance in other ways. Apart from root damage to concrete or plastic pool liners, excessive leaf drop at the end of summer tends to clog the water, setting up a biological chain of decomposition that quickly turns the water rank. The only solution is unattractive netting – impractical anyway over large areas – or conscientious trawl-

RIGHT *Trees and water are perfect companions when a specimen near the water's edge makes interesting colours and patterns on the surface of a pool or where a nearby group is cleverly reflected in all its autumn glory like a Persian carpet. At Stourhead in England, trees such as beech (*Fagus sylvatica*), small* Carpinus betulus *and tall* Thuja occidentalis *have been planted on a slight rise to catch their reflection in the adjoining lake.*

BELOW *Beside a large pond or lake, trees must be strong enough visually to compete with bold marginal planting like the giant* Gunnera manicata. *Here a couple of swamp cypresses (*Taxodium distichum*) add valuable height to the scheme, their strong pyramidal shape and fine foliage the perfect contrast to the fleshy waterside plants.*

RIGHT *The Golden Weeping Willow (*Salix × chrysocoma*) is the classic water-side tree, frequently seen dipping its great shaggy head into streams and rivers. It can grow a little too large for most gardens but here it has been planted at a distance from a small formal pool where its delicate trailing branches can still hang over the water and provide dappled shade. In contrast to its light featheriness, tightly clipped box trees stand guard at the corners of the pool.*

ABOVE *Without its sentinel oaks (*Quercus robur*) forming an archway through which the water seems to flow, this formal pool would look rather dull and one-dimensional. The trees do not just give the area added height and breadth, but liven up the other-wise bare surface of the water with their reflected leaves and branches.*

ing and dredging which disturbs water plants and wildlife. The shade cast by the canopy of foliage can be a problem, as too much of it will inhibit plant growth. The best and most suitable trees for the water's edge are deciduous: most conifers are too dark and tall for anything smaller than a lake and needle drop can poison the water.

The ideal trees to plant near water are those with a light leaf canopy producing dappled shade. The water-lovers like the willows (*Salix*), which like to grow with their roots submerged in water, have delicately cut or strongly-coloured foliage, making them particularly suitable because of the wonderful reflections they make.

One of the loveliest is the Golden Weeping Willow (*Salix* × *chrysocoma*) with its graceful golden branches trailing in the water or the interesting Corkscrew or Dragon's Claw Willow (*Salix matsudana* 'Tortuosa') whose contorted branches make it a fascinating spectacle all year, with the bonus of silver catkins in spring.

Other trees will have to be planted slightly back from the water's edge in better-drained soil or on raised banks. Here too a dwarfed or drooping habit looks particularly effective, the branches leaning towards the water as if to admire their own reflection. Many of the natural water's-edge trees have dangling catkins which add to the effect, swinging like green or golden tassels in the water's sparkle. One such is the alder, hardy and fast-growing, which produces catkins in early spring at a time when there is little else of interest. The Common Alder (*Alnus glutinosa*) tends to be rather invasive, but a more decorative variety, like the cut-leaved *A. incana* 'Laciniata', makes a pretty pool-side tree and has a more better habit.

Another suitable catkin tree is the birch, combining light foliage with interesting bark and in spring, fat lambs' tails hanging from its branches. One of the best is *Betula pendula* with its weeping form and beautiful peeling silver-white bark.

However, for decorative value, the ornamental maples are unbeatable. The Ash-Leaved Maple or Box Elder (*Acer negundo*) with its yellow-green tufts of flowers and yellow autumn colour would brighten any pool side. For smaller pools, the dwarf cultivar *A. palmatum* 'Dissectum' is ideal, leaning its feathery foliage towards the water.

Seaside Gardens

Like sea birds and saltwater fish, all plants, and particularly trees, need to be specially adapted to survive in the exacting conditions of coastal regions. Seaside gardens can be difficult to establish; they are subjected to the remorseless glare of sun on water and lashed by salty winds and strong gales that distort and stunt the sturdiest of trees; even the soil tends to be thin, sandy and undernourished. However much you may enjoy the spectacular view of the bay, your garden plants will prefer the protection of wind- (and salt-) resistant trees like the Monterey Pine (*Pinus radiata*). Better still, sturdy screening will shelter both trees and smaller plants. Leave gaps or 'windows' in screening or tree planting to retain selected views of vistas.

There are trees that are tolerant of sand and salt and put on a brave display in prevailing winds: mulberries and rowans, for example, which both have an attractive shape, interesting foliage and coloured fruits, although the mulberry (*Morus nigra*) is rather a slow grower. The large-leaved *Paulownia imperialis* also puts up with salt and sand but the flower buds may be damaged by cold winds so it does need some shelter. It produces dense foliage and some welcome shade as a result.

BELOW *Dense background screening need not obscure a lovely view but can be planned to frame it as a focal point without losing any of its protective benefits. This beautiful backdrop is full of interest and allows a glimpse of water and mountains beyond between the light spreading foliage of a tall plane tree and the sturdy dark green pyramid of* Picea abies. *Dense-foliaged shrubs in shades of gold, bronze and green bring the arrangement right down to ground level.*

Another excellent slow grower, resistant to wind damage and effective as screening, is the Holm Oak (*Quercus ilex*) – a spreading evergreen that prefers well-drained soil.

Other good trees for sandy soil and exposed conditions include the hardy Maritime or Cluster Pine (*Pinus pinaster*) and the Grey Poplar (*Populus canescens*). Other survivors include the horse-chestnuts and buckeyes (*Aesculus*), whitebeams, white poplars and, surprisingly, a member of the pear family, the Snow Pear (*Pyrus nivalis*) which has pretty grey foliage and attractive flowers, with the bonus of tiny pear-like fruits. Other trees worth considering are the Sweet Gum (*Liquidambar styraciflua*), which tolerates salt but not a windy site. Another tough coastal tree is the Common Hawthorn (*Crataegus monogyna*).

In the right climate, there are many Mediterranean species (see page 34) whose needle-like foliage and grey coloration (a protective waxy bloom) are ideally suited to conserving moisture and withstanding strong breezes: *Eucalyptus* is tender but Juniper is hardy on most sites.

To keep sandy soil together, and provide some good low-level screening, include strong background planting. The Sea Buckthorn (*Hippophae rhamnoides*) is a natural subject for a seaside garden as its name suggests. It can be trained into a tree, some 9 m (30 ft) high or left as a large shrub to flesh out the tree planting. Its silvery leaves catch the light in the wind and it produces attractive orange berries in autumn. Other tough large shrubs are *Escallonia*, *Olearia* and shrub roses. One of the best of the latter for seaside gardens is *Rosa* 'Nevada'.

LEFT *The strong black branches and flat dark head of the Stone Pine (*Pinus pinea*) shout 'seaside' as loudly as any striped beach parasol. It is a common sight in the Mediterranean where it is popular for its dramatic architectural shape, but the tree is surprisingly hardy and makes an excellent salt- and wind-resistant specimen in a more temperate climate.*

Mediterranean Gardens

The shimmering, hot dry atmosphere of the Mediterranean climate has its own distinctive colours and textures, typified by woolly greys, soft mauves, olive greens and the hazy impression of fleshy leaves, tassels and feathers – all designed to minimize moisture loss. No sight is more evocative of the Mediterranean than hillsides dotted with the compact blue, green and grey forms of pine, cypress, juniper, olive and fig. These are trees with a high oil content and a strong scent released by hot sunshine to blend with the aroma of the smaller plants below: grey and purple plants like lavender and rosemary.

In more temperate climates, hardier varieties of such plants and trees will create their own miniature hot, dry atmosphere in a sunny corner of the garden, humming with insects and heavy with scent. A sheltered grouping of more tender Mediterranean trees and plants like *Buddleia alternifolia* and *Oleander aerium* can be grown in tubs on the patio, and brought inside should the temperature fall below freezing.

In the Mediterranean garden, trees are essential for shade and screening from prevailing winds; blend the hues of the blue-green Atlas or Atlantic Cedar (*Cedrus atlantica* 'Glauca'), deep green umbrella of the Stone Pine (*Pinus pinea*), and the dark green, almost black firs or Golden Irish Yew (*Taxus baccata* 'Fastigiata Aurea').

RIGHT *Greys, greens, mauves and blues typify the Mediterranean landscape. These small olive trees are perfectly at home in a field of lavender on a south-facing slope, making a subtle blend of colours that is easy on the eye when the light is bright, and releasing a heady perfume in the heat of the sun. Because the trees are small with round compact heads of silver-grey foliage, they can be planted in uneven groups to concentrate the effect of their attractive colour and leaf shape.*

ABOVE *These* Lagerstroemia indica *with their splendid pink flowers and fern-like foliage have been grown as small standards along the approach to the house to make a spectacular avenue. Strong shapes and colours are ideally suited to a deep blue sky and stark white painted buildings.*

LEFT *The magnificent cloud of pink produced by the Judas Tree (*Cercis siliquastrum*) in full bloom looks perfect amongst grey-leaved shrubs and trees and the occasional dark, sculptural evergreen.*

—*II*—

The Special Features of Trees

Trees have an astonishing diversity of attractive characteristics – many of them not fully appreciated, such as beautiful bark effects or interesting branch forms – which can add immeasurably to the appearance of the garden in winter when the herbaceous planting is dying down. The leaves of many of the deciduous trees can bring a rich and exciting new dimension to the garden in autumn, while the massed displays of flowers of *Malus* or *Prunus* have an almost magical effect in early spring. At the back of the book, on page 190, there are lists of the best trees for particular effects – autumn foliage colour, all-seasons appeal, spring and summer flowers, evergreen leaves, and so on.

Cornus controversa *at leaf fall*

Foliage Colour

It is easy to forget the dominant part foliage colour plays when choosing garden trees but even a single tree can provide a fascinating spectrum of colours as the seasons change. Every specimen must be judged in relation to its neighbours right through the year to ensure a good balance of leaf colours and to avoid any jarring combinations, such as a tree with lime-green or strong yellow foliage against some of the brighter pink ornamental Japanese cherries. You should try to avoid the lopsided effect produced by planting all the gold-turning trees on one side of the garden with all the scarlet- and purple-turning ones on the other.

In the larger garden, a background framework of a variety of dark green evergreens will temper the brighter colours and provide a good backdrop, but with a small plot, the trees will have to be chosen to offer maximum interest throughout the year: a single tree of *Gleditsia triacanthos* 'Sunburst' in front of a curve of, say, five *Carpinus betulus* 'Columnaris', or alternatively a *Sorbus aria* 'Mitchellii' with a *Prunus subhirtella* 'Autumnalis', producing a blend of shapes with flowers in spring, attractive foliage in summer and autumn colour. Rowans, larches (*Larix*) and the ornamental maples (*Acer*) all supply fine foliage colours throughout the year together with interesting leaf shape and particularly graceful habit.

Take your garden season by season to work out how foliage colours will blend together or with surrounding plant colours. In spring the garden often relies on the fresh lime-green or golden-yellow leaves of trees like the Golden Weeping Willow (*Salix × chrysocoma*) but some trees also have pink or reddish new growth – *Acer pseudo-*

LEFT *Trees with bright, almost golden foliage like this* Gleditsia triacanthos *'Sunburst' do an excellent job brightening up a dull corner or drawing the eye towards another part of the garden. Note how the golden colour is emphasized by being picked up by ground-cover plants below.*

ABOVE *A beautiful arrangement of foliage shape and colour, producing a backcloth of greens and creams for a semi-formal garden. Pride of place is given to the variegated foliage of* Cornus controversa *'Variegata' that has been given room to spread itself against the darker green trees behind.*

platanus 'Brilliantissimum' is pink and later turns yellow-green. In spring, it looks very lovely against the pale green of emerging larch needles or the newly opened leaves of the Dawyck Beech (*Fagus sylvatica* 'Dawyck').

In summer as the foliage matures, the garden is transformed under a canopy in a myriad shades of green, but again some trees will produce more unusual colours which are useful for eye-catching contrast.

The yellow-leaved Indian Bean Tree (*Catalpa bignonioides* 'Aurea') is prized for its wonderful golden colour and the Golden Monterey Cypress (*Cupressus macrocarpa* 'Goldcrest') will add a sunny touch among duller greens. Golden-leaved trees look good when blended with the subtle silver-grey of the Silver Willow (*Salix alba* 'Sericea'), the hardy Oleaster (*Elaeagnus angustifolia*) or the Weeping Silver Lime (*Tilia* 'Petiolaris').

Reds and purples add a dramatic note and should be used sparingly, especially in small gardens, but the delicate *Acer palmatum* 'Dissectum Atropurpureum' with its trailing branches of feathery purple foliage is tiny enough not to overpower the smallest border. Larger areas can play host to *Cotinus coggygria* 'Purpureus' or, on a grander scale, a spectacular large dense-headed Rivers Purple Beech (*Fagus sylvatica* 'Riversii').

There are several trees with attractive cream or white variegated leaves including some of the dogwoods (*Cornus*), the creamy-white and green Angelica Tree (*Aralia elata* 'Variegata'), which needs shelter, and many of the hollies (*Ilex spp*).

As the year wanes and deciduous foliage starts to die off, the well-planned garden flames with colour. The Japanese maples (*Acer palmatum*) are the champions here, perfectly bred for smaller gardens and covered extensively in other sections, but you might also like to enjoy the brilliant gold-yellow linden (*Tilia*), orange or scarlet rowan (*Sorbus*) or the large, pollution-resistant Maidenhair Tree (*Ginkgo biloba*) whose green fan-shaped leaves with yellow edges are superb in autumn.

You can blend several of these colours into a rich autumn tapestry providing the trees are close enough. A few sombre evergreens (see page 184) among them can help to pull the colours together.

LEFT *Judicious use of blue can be a real eye-catcher in a garden of more sombre evergreens. Here* Picea pungens glauca *'Kosteri Pendula' provides foreground interest against a background of trees including* Cedrus deodara *and* Thuja occidentalis.

ABOVE *The evergreens include some useful golden colours among the more familiar blues and greens.* Taxus baccata *'Semperaurea' is doubly valuable for its evergreen bright colour and its smaller, more informal shape against stately pyramids and cones.*

A single specimen or, better still, a small grove of Japanese maples will set your garden on fire with colour at the end of summer when other plants have finished. The effect of these Acer palmatum heptalobum *'Osakazuki' is perfectly breath-taking both in the branches and in the fallen leaves below, making an attractive multi-coloured carpet.*

SHAPE & FORM

UNLESS IT IS artificially distorted by clipping or training, or by adverse weather conditions, every tree at maturity forms a quite distinct size and shape, whether it be tall and conical (columnar); pyramidal; short, squat and round-headed, or weeping. Trees tend to look very alike as saplings, so it is very important when choosing individual species and varieties in a garden centre to know what their ultimate size and outline, as well as their foliage shape and colour, will be. It is worth visiting any attractively planted parks, large gardens or arboreta to see mature specimens planted *in situ*.

The shape of a tree is important in relation to its intended position; where space is restricted, for example, avoid a form with invasive branches and choose a tall narrow tree like *Acer platanoides* 'Columnare', *Ilex × altaclarensis* 'Camelliifolia' or *Malus baccata* 'Columnaris'. For an area where a tree has plenty of room to spread and where the shade it casts presents no problem, you can indulge yourself with one of the generously proportioned round-headed forms: maybe a handsome large-leaved Indian Bean Tree (*Catalpa bignonioides*) or the Japanese Crab Apple (*Malus floribunda*), the attractive light foliage of which might cast welcome dappled shade over a garden bench.

Any group of trees will look better if it contains a contrast of shapes; put the tall, columnar trees at the rear with lower, round-headed or weeping varieties in front. In a small garden a group of just three can provide a surprising degree of variety and interest – take, for example, a tall dark green (turning yellow later) hornbeam (*Carpinus betulus* 'Columnaris') flanked by a wide-spreading *Acer pseudoplatanus* 'Brilliantissimum' with its golden-tinted foliage and an *Acer palmatum* 'Dissectum', chosen for its dome-like shape and particularly fine, feathery leaves.

The formal garden at Drummond Castle in Scotland demonstrates the tremendous variety and scope available using clipped and shaped trees and a wide spectrum of foliage colours. The layout follows the design of the national flag – a saltire cross – with trees and annual planting providing the correct colours. Here there are great pyramids and domes of clipped yew, formal hedges of box and yew, lollipops, cones and fan shapes using green- and bronze-leaved maples and a lovely Fagus sylvatica *'Purpurea'.*

Columnar trees

Often the very shape of a particular tree will suggest where it might look best or spark off an interesting design idea. The classic column-forming trees like poplars have an elegant, stately air about them, making them ideal subjects in formal gardens, for pairing on either side of an entrance or to draw the eye to a good viewing point. Alternatively they can be grouped to rise majestically at the rear of other species. Columnar poplars of particular interest include the White Poplar (*Populus alba* 'Pyramidalis'), which has an eye-catching silvery-white sheen to the foliage and good yellow autumn colour, and the fast-growing Lombardy Poplar (*Populus nigra* 'Italica') which makes useful screening. *Acer saccharum* 'Temple's Upright' eventually makes a tall column of wonderful lobed leaves that turn fiery orange at the end of summer.

Trees with their branches neatly displayed upwards in joyful supplication are always a cheery sight; the Lombardy Poplars are narrow and erect, making them a good choice as screening or path-

LEFT *Dark green evergreens – here dramatic columns of* Taxus baccata *'Fastigiata' – are an excellent foil for brighter, spikier or more decorative foliage patterns. The framework for this bright flower garden is balanced by the deep green foliage of the Holm Oak (*Quercus ilex*).*

BELOW *You will find a wide scope of shapes and sizes within a single genus. The familiar wide-spreading, shady oak may also make tall, narrower columnar shapes in gardens where height rather than width is needed, like this upright Oak (*Quercus robur *'Fastigiata').*

ABOVE *You can distract the eye from a less than interesting view with something a little unusual like this low spreading* Rhus typhina *'Laciniata'. Its twisting horizontal dark branches and unusual fern-like foliage make it an excellent specimen tree, striking a well-weathered mature attitude that would be equally suitable for an oriental setting.*

ABOVE *There is no mistaking the magnificent domed shape of the regal Beech and it is worth giving it space to spread itself on a large lawn, particularly if it is one of the fine copper- or purple-coloured varieties like this* Fagus sylvatica *'Purpurea'.*

side trees. This is the most useful group of shapes for a small garden and includes the narrow forms of Lawson Cypress (*Chamaecyparis lawsoniana* 'Columnaris') and the upright Rowan (*Sorbus aucuparia* 'Sheerwater Seedling').

Spreading and pyramidal trees

Save the Japanese maples (*Acer palmatum*), Japanese cherries (*Prunus*) and the crab apples (*Malus*) for a site where they can spread their lovely branches and where you can enjoy the benefits of the light shade provided. As a specimen tree in the centre of a lawn or used to create a shady bower or patio, these, and others like many of the dogwoods (*Cornus*) and the Cockspur Hawthorn (*Crataegus crus-galli*), contribute splendid blossom, as well as good foliage shape and colour.

There are also many trees which have a good spread of branches but which produce more of a defined, rounded or pyramidal shape, again useful as a focal point, for shade and as a more formal element without your scheme. Such trees tend to be on the large side, but they can be really spectacular in a setting large enough to do them justice; a mature oak (*Quercus robur*) or the fast-growing Norway Maple (*Acer platanoides*). These are trees with a dense canopy of foliage producing heavy shade, so it is difficult to grow anything much beneath them.

Weeping trees

There are also weeping or pendular forms of many tree species – not all of them as successful as weeping willows (*Salix*) or birches (*Betula pendula* 'Youngii') which look so lovely trailing their branches over water. Keep to the tried and tested favourites like the small Weeping Purple Beech (*Fagus sylvatica* 'Purpurea Pendula') or the even smaller *Acer palmatum* 'Dissectum Atropurpureum' as a focal point to your plan.

LEFT *(main picture) Trees never cease to surprise with their vast range of shapes and sizes, providing complementary and contrasting groupings even within a relatively small area. Clumps of feathery bamboo crouch at the foot of a mighty-stemmed* Taxodium, *itself a contrast with the nearby weeping beech (* Fagus sylvatica *'Pendula') like a green fountain and another weeping form – this time a deep purple beech (* F. sylvatica *'Purpurea Pendula').*

INSET *Many of the Japanese maples have been specially bred to suit smaller gardens or to provide an eye-catching focal point in a corner of a large one. In* Acer palmatum *'Dissectum', every covetable attribute seems combined in the one tree: little bigger than a shrub, it has exquisite finely cut leaves and first-class autumn colour as well as a compact mound-forming habit.*

ABOVE *Weeping or pendulous trees can contribute interesting shapes to your general scheme, but a species like this* Prunus *(* P. × yedoensis *'Ivensii'), is worthy of a prime position as a focal point for the fine display it makes.*

BARK, STEMS & ROOTS

BARK IS OFTEN forgotten when the merits of a particular tree are considered. Yet the variety of colour, texture and pattern in different tree barks is quite outstanding and can make a positive contribution to a garden design when blending colours or planning special features. Think of the ghostly qualities of a group of silver birches (*Betula pendula*) in the fading gleam of dusk, or the strong statement made by the single shiny red-brown trunk of a Tibetan Cherry (*Prunus serrula*).

If you plant a group of the same type of trees together, you will find that a hint of white, grey or russet in a bark will strengthen to a stronger swathe of colour in vertical bands of light and shade. Eucalyptus and Grey Poplar are good examples of trees with light speckled bark that are useful for adding light to an otherwise dark area, while the rich red of many of the cherries and maples adds warmth and colour to a dull garden. Some bark is so spectacular that it deserves to be made a special feature. A specimen tree of the Chinese Stewartia (*Stewartia sinensis*), for example, with its exotic peeling pink-red bark or the Red Snake-bark Maple (*Acer capillipes*), with its distinctive lime-green markings will always attract comment in a carefully chosen focal point, such as the centre of a lawn.

Once you start looking more closely at the trunk, and not just at the leaves, flowers and fruits of your trees, you will begin to understand the scope they can offer the discerning landscaper. Even the more familiar species may surprise you: the chocolate-flake-like twisted ridges of the Sweet Chestnut (*Castanea sativa*), for example, or the piebald patches of a London Plane (*Platanus × acerifolia*). A peeling or flaking bark adds interest to any ornamental tree and the best known example is the Paperbark Maple (*Acer griseum*), which only grows to 4.5-6 m (15-20 ft) and has a magnificent bark of copper-bronze and pinkish-red that hangs in great sheets and curls. The Paperbark Maple has the bonus of superb autumn colour, but the Strawberry Tree (*Arbutus unedo*) is equally useful for its evergreen leaves and peeling dark brown bark or, in the case of the less hardy *Arbutus menziesii*, reddish-orange bark. Another handsome tree whose bark hangs in fine

ABOVE *This variety of the Paper or Canoe Birch (*Betula papyrifera*) peels off its parchment-like bark to reveal a copper trunk – a silver and copper combination guaranteed to brighten the garden right through the year.*

RIGHT *(main picture) A tree with rough furrowed bark like this Douglas Fir (*Pseudotsuga menziesii*) offers infinite variations of colour and pattern and a good textural contrast with trees with smoother shiny bark. The subtle colours are interesting in themselves: browns, greens and even turquoise.*

RIGHT *(inset top) The glossy trunks of a maple are a perfect colour match for the rough stone wall behind, but provide an interesting contrast of textures. (Inset below) The marbled bark of this* Eucalyptus *looks almost surreal with great swirls of creamy-white on grey.*

RIGHT *Soil often gets washed away on a sloping site, leaving the roots of any trees exposed. Here an ancient beech (*Fagus sylvatica*) has made weird and wonderful shapes both above and below. The roots make an interesting feature over an area too shady even for grass to grow.*

CENTRE *Training trees to grow with their roots entwined around a rock is a popular bonsai technique: here nature has done the job herself in a full-size woodland, creating a stunning feature out of this old yew (*Taxus baccata*) whose root system is exposed clinging to a High Weald sandstone outcrop at Wakehurst Place in Sussex, England.*

tatters is the Paper Birch (*Betula papyrifera*), whose white bark has interesting varied orange, pink or dark brown markings.

Roots

You probably never think of roots as one of a tree's more decorative features. They usually serve their purpose unseen, stabilizing and nourishing the trunk and branches underground, and sometimes making their presence known by interfering with water pipes or the roots of surrounding shrubs or other trees.

But there are some species which throw up aerial roots that snake along the surface of the ground and make an interesting gnarled feature, particularly in situations where little else might grow: in the shade of large branches, for example. Most famous of these is the Swamp Cypress (*Taxodium distichum*) which surrounds itself with a knobbly mass of bumps and roots and which prefers a boggy, even waterlogged, location, although it will also grow in drier soils. The Swamp Cypress looks particularly good growing beside an informal pond or pool where the roots stretching out into the shallows provide useful year-round interest.

You will often find that other pond-side trees like willow and birch start to expose their roots as the bank erodes and slips away, making an attractive additional feature; you might also see exposed roots beneath spreading species like sweet chestnuts or beeches whose mature dense canopy allows little to grow (not even grass) and where rainwater sometimes washes away the bare soil leaving the roots exposed. Providing you take care not to damage the roots when mowing surrounding lawn, they can make a fascinating feature in a large garden.

Exposed beech roots again – this time of Fagus americana *whose long grey toes seem to rummage in the russet leaves at the foot of this great tree.*

FLOWERS & SCENT

LEFT Eucryphia × nymansensis *'Nymansay' is a tall hybrid which produces the loveliest translucent flowers with golden stamens in late summer. It is extremely prolific, producing a mass of blooms over the whole tree and offering spectacular contrast against the glossy evergreen foliage.*

RIGHT *With its long scented racemes of flowers that hang down like a curtain,* Wisteria *is popular for training over arbours and walkways. The white form* W. macrobotrys *'Alba' is particularly beautiful but rarely seen. More common is the mauve or purple Wisteria (*W. sinensis *- inset) which is also an excellent subject for training along wires or poles to display the blossom more clearly.*

A TREE in full bloom is an awe-inspiring sight: its very size and height produce a striking cloud of shape and colour and an ever-changing effect according to the colour of the sky behind or the movement of the wind.

There is a flowering tree for every season of the year, but late winter to early spring, when there is little else around, is when a show of blossom is most welcome. The familiar whites and pinks of the flowering cherries like the Spring Cherry (*Prunus subhirtella*), the Flowering Dogwood (*Cornus florida*), various forms of *Magnolia* and many of the ornamental thorns (*Crataegus*) and crab apples (*Malus*) are not the only spring colours at your command. Experiment with yellow by planting a Laburnum (small but short-lived) or, if you have the room, a Cornelian Cherry (*Cornus mas*); add a dash of scarlet with pretty *Crataegus oxyacantha* 'Paul's Scarlet' or *Malus* 'Profusion', or even a subtle mauve or purple to offset the mauves and yellows of spring bulbs below. The Eastern Redbud (*Cercis canadensis*) covers its branches with tiny purple flowers; the beautiful *Paulownia tomentosa* will produce a wealth of mauve foxglove- or hyacinth-like flowers with a vanilla scent.

These spring-flowering trees should be positioned where you can enjoy them from the house and scented species should be placed close to a path or patio where their fragrance can be best appreciated. For showy blooms and a subtle scent, a flowering tree like *Magnolia × soulangiana* is worth looking forward to all winter and even the smallest garden or patio has room for a tiny *Magnolia stellata* with its small scented star-shaped flowers.

You will find that many summer-flowering trees, like *Magnolia wilsonii*, are sweetly scented to add to their charms. Position the lovely hanging racemes of *Cladrastis lutea*, the small Snowbell (*Styrax japonica*) or Lilac (*Syringa reticulata*) close

to your patio or seating area where you can enjoy both the sight and scent of their lovely blooms.

There are trees such as *Eucryphia* which bloom later, in summer or even late into autumn, when they can produce an unexpected display above late summer flowers or among autumn foliage. In fact the majority of late-flowering trees have white flowers which have a useful fresh, 'lightening' effect against the hotter shades of bedding plants or the reds, oranges and golds of changing leaves. One of the exceptions is the popular Autumn Cherry (*Prunus subhirtella* 'Autumnalis Rosea') which has pink flowers; another is the sunny yellow of the Tree of Heaven (*Ailanthus altissima*).

Some trees, such as crab apples, ornamental cherries and short-lived trees like *Laburnum*, may flower when only two or three years old, but with the majority you will have to wait until they approach maturity.

LEFT *Trees with white blossom in the early spring have a brightening effect against dark branches and still wintry skies and are easier on the eye than some of the brighter pinks. If you have room for several trees, mix white with pink varieties for a more subtle harmony. These lovely dense flower clusters are the product of* Prunus avium *'Plena'.*

LEFT *The Indian Bean Tree (*Catalpa bignonioides*) is one of the most spectacular trees to flower, producing clusters of orchid-like trumpets, a frilled white exterior spotted with purple and yellow tongues inside. This is a tree with excellent foliage and fruits too, but it requires plenty of space to spread itself and a rich moist soil.*

LEFT Prunus sargentii *makes an excellent specimen tree, producing both a spectacular display of blossom in spring and exquisite fiery autumn foliage colour.*

RIGHT *The beautiful flowering cherry (*Prunus subhirtella *'Pendula') smothers its branches with pink blossoms before the leaves are really out in spring, making a superb focal point in a small garden.*

ORNAMENTAL FRUITS

Luscious edible fruits have a short season of ripeness then drop to the ground and rot if not picked and eaten. Yet trees with ornamental fruits and berries often put on a brave display of colour and interest from late summer through to the following spring if not first plundered by birds. Perhaps it is the contrast of gold or scarlet fruit against glossy green evergreen leaves or bare branches that makes them seem so rich and brilliant, but our anticipation as fruits slowly change colour is always well rewarded. The heavy-fruiting *Sorbus*, *Malus* or *Crataegus* make a spread of gold or orange among autumn foliage; and a holly (*Ilex*) with a full head of scarlet berries against winter snow is always a magnificent sight.

Trees with interesting fruits are especially important in small gardens for the extra interest they can provide, particularly on smaller species like certain rowans (*Sorbus*), crab apples (*Malus*) and cherry trees (*Prunus*) which can offer interesting summer foliage, spring blossom and good autumn colour too. However, it is not a good idea to plant trees with prolific fruits and berries too close to the patio or any other paved area, as they do make a mess and sometimes stain.

The familiar round and oval fruits and berries mentioned, in shades of yellow, red and orange, make a useful splash of colour in the large garden or a late-season focal point in a small one, but there are trees with more unusual fruits or prominent seeds that are well worth hunting out. The hardy Japanese Snowbell (*Styrax japonica*) follows its white summer trumpets with green fruits; the Dove or Handkerchief Tree (*Davidia involucrata*) – an excellent specimen tree at around 6-12 m (20-40 ft) – has green fruits like giant gooseberries. There are trees with dramatic black or dark purple fruits, like the Amur Cork Tree (*Phellodendron amurense*) which is worth growing

LEFT *The Yew (*Taxus baccata*) produces unusual waxy red and green berries that look rather like stuffed olives in reverse. They are very attractive but highly poisonous.*

RIGHT *A profusion of vivid scarlet berries adorns* Cotoneaster *'Hybridus Pendulus' even after the frosts. One of the finest of the larger-growing cotoneasters, it can be trained into tree-like form by pruning and makes a valuable specimen tree for any small garden.*

LEFT *Some hybrids have bright yellow berries rather than the more usual red and orange, which are useful for creating colour contrasts in autumn and winter. This particular species of crab apple,* Malus *'Golden Hornet', is a fine tree for small gardens. It has attractive foliage and the golden fruits often remain on the bare branches right through winter.*

LEFT *From the top left, clockwise: these strange-looking fruits belong to the Blue Gum (*Eucalyptus globulus*) and have a grey-blue bloom to them as do the leaves. The Indian Bean Tree (*Catalpa bignonioides*) gets its name from the long narrow seed pods which do look very like beans, clustered among the large flat leaves. The Goat Willow (*Salix caprea*) produces some of the prettiest catkins – bright yellow bottle brushes in spring. These large catkins are male; the female ones are smaller and silver-grey. The Atlas Cedar (*Cedrus atlantica*) has particularly attractive cones, of a soft grey-green colour like the foliage and a tightly whorled barrel shape.*

anyway for its delicate foliage, and the hardy Tupelo or Black Gum (*Nyssa sylvatica*) whose clusters of black berries have a blue bloom.

Don't forget that trees also provide us with our more unusual and interesting fruit and seed shapes in the garden. The winged seeds of the Sycamore are probably already familiar and a great favourite with children as they spin on the wind; better suited to gardens, with the same winged seeds or 'keys' in rosy-pink or red, is the far more modest Amur Maple (*Acer ginnala*). The Sweet Gum (*Liquidambar styraciflua*) produces wonderful (but sometimes messy) browny-green spiky sputniks, as well as fine autumn colour, particularly *L.s.* 'Variegata', whose yellow foliage turns deep rosy-pink in autumn. For an exotic oriental touch add a tender Golden Rain Tree (*Koelreuteria paniculata*) whose excellent coloured foliage and spectacular golden display of flowers is followed by green, later to turn pink, lanterns.

Equally interesting are the cones produced by a number of conifers.

—III—

TREES FOR A PURPOSE

Gardeners frequently neglect trees when choosing plants for the garden, often out of ignorance of the many species and varieties now available. Trees have a valuable role to play in the garden, both in aesthetic and practical terms. They can be used to provide shelter or much-needed shade, will sometimes provide a wonderful crop of delicious but less familiar fruit, or can be used as an architectural element in a garden that has no other vertical features. Here we look at the many different applications of trees, and some of best species and cultivars available for a variety of special purposes.

An avenue of horse chestnuts
(Aesculus hippocastanum)

Specimen Trees

A SPECIMEN TREE is simply one that is either attractive or interesting enough, preferably throughout the year, to merit being singled out for a special position. It can take pride of place for various reasons: by catching the eye with a spread of vibrant colour, spectacular leaf shape, or striking form.

To draw attention to such a tree, you must think carefully about where you are siting it. Make sure that any background foliage is complementary and that there is enough room around the tree to enjoy its assets to the full.

In a small garden particularly, do not be seduced by a tree of spectacular but limited charms. Some of the Japanese ornamental cherries, for example, while producing a wonderful display of blossom for a short period, have little else to recommend them. Opt instead for one like *Prunus sargentii* which has spring flowers, summer fruits and strong autumn colour.

Other strong contenders would be a rowan like *Sorbus* 'Joseph Rock' with its feathery foliage and bright yellow berries; the crab apple *Malus* 'John Downie' with both flowers and fruit or the Paperbark Maple (*Acer griseum*) with its orange peeling bark, yellow spring leaves and flowers that turn green and then red. Similarly effective would be the Cockspur Thorn (*Crataegus crus-galli*) with purple shoots, white flowers, red fruits and good autumn colour or the compact holly (*Ilex aquifolium* 'Pyramidalis') which produces a mass of red berries in winter.

LEFT *This superb evergreen Holm Oak (*Quercus ilex*) has been incorporated into a formal parterre of clipped box (*Buxus sempervirens*) and itself trimmed into a neat dome to take a starring role among neat hedges and trimmed yews.*

RIGHT *Sometimes a magnificent specimen tree is worth keeping despite its advanced years and you may have to plan your garden round it. This gnarled but noble *Pinus sylvestris* demands a prime position where the lawn meets a patio and a new pool. A few plants in pots are arranged close by to keep it company and to make a more interesting setting, for only grass will grow beneath its dense canopy.*

Equally, you could grow one of the more unusual and attractive fruit trees: a medlar (*Mespilus germanica*) with its sprawling, rather crooked habit, large white spring flowers and brown fruit in autumn or the Black Mulberry (*Morus nigra*). Both like a sunny site and each could stand alone in a small lawn.

With more space, you have scope for more dramatic effects, using larger trees like the handsome Black Pine (*Pinus nigra*), the fresh lime-green Maidenhair Tree (*Ginkgo biloba*), a Walnut (*Juglans regia*) or a Monterey Cypress with its huge dominating head of dark foliage. The magnificent oaks, chestnuts and buckeyes with their dense pyramidal shapes and dramatic stature are good subjects as centrepieces of a large lawn.

There are many different ways of drawing attention to a specimen tree. It can provide the only vertical interest in an expanse of well-mown grass; it can stand alone in a formal hard-surfaced garden, surrounded by pebbles or gravel; it can catch the eye as the centrepiece in a traditional knot garden. In a border it can also draw the eye towards the sky, with a line of larger shrubs leading the eye up to it. If the best feature of a specimen tree needs to be seen close to – for example the peeling bark – make sure that nearby shrub planting does not obscure it. Similarly, if the tree's outstanding virtue is the way its silvery leaves catch the light when rustled by the breeze, give it a position where its true glory can be properly appreciated.

The backdrop to a specimen tree should be taken into account before making your choice to set off a particularly strong colour to best advantage; any of the golden-leaved trees will look good against a background of dark evergreens; the stronger-coloured, purple-leaved trees need siting with care if they are not to dominate the rest of the planting or clash with it.

Any underplanting of specimen trees should be planned to complement the tree. For the greatest impact choose a single species that must, of course, be shade-tolerant. In a town front garden, a small purple-leaved acer (*Acer palmatum* 'Dissectum Atropurpureum') would look good surrounded by the spreading ground cover of the purple-leaved *Viola labradorica*, for example.

Their branches positively weighed down with blossom in spring, a pair of Prunus avium *'Plena' has been sited on a slight slope so that their canopy of dark branches and snow-white blossom can dominate the garden. The trees can be enjoyed from behind and below as well as from the front, where nothing can be seen but a curtain of flowers.*

SCREENING

SHELTER NOT ONLY makes your garden a much more private place, it also alters the micro-climate, making it possible to grow a wider range of plants than you would normally be able to. Although walls and fences are an effective means of protecting the garden boundaries – sometimes the only way in exposed areas – trees and large shrubs make excellent natural screening at a higher level, eventually, than any wall or fence. They do demand more in the way of maintenance but they have the bonus of variety of colour, form and texture as well as height. In a smaller garden, it increases the scope for planting and gives it vertical interest. Carefully chosen, trees and shrubs offer a great deal more visually than a straight line of walling or fencing, particularly if species are mixed and slightly staggered when planted. Although the best screening trees are evergreens, many of the conifers are dull – an unrelieved row of Leyland cypresses, although fast-growing and very wind-resistant, do not offer much visual excitement. You would be far better off with a mixture of deciduous and evergreen subjects – the Common Beech (*Fagus sylvatica*) and Whitebeam (*Sorbus aria*) with evergreen hollies (*Ilex*) and White Cedar (*Thuja occidentalis*), for example. Plant some lowerstorey shrubs to provide screening at the base. By

ABOVE *An excellent example of how mixed screening works best on several levels. A low clipped hedge of beech divides the more formal flower garden from a wooded area of broad-leaved trees behind. Against this backdrop of greys and greens, the brighter flowering shrubs are reserved for the forefront. Using trees and shrubs to divide the garden into compartments in this way makes it more intimate and more enjoyable.*

RIGHT *The owner of this slightly sloping garden was lucky enough to have a mature backdrop of established trees. This has been reinforced with the thick belt of bright green foliage of* Prunus cerasifera *'Pissardii', graduating downwards to brighter flowering shrubs and the occasional dwarf conifer to give height to the herbaceous borders.*

mixing species in this way, you get variations in leaf colour and changing colours throughout the year. In a town garden, you would be well advised to choose erect, columnar trees that are not going to cause problems with overhanging branches. Alternatively, use trees that can be pruned or clipped to keep them under control.

When planting a mixed group, it is best to put them about 2 m (6 ft 6 in) apart in staggered blocks of uneven numbers. This filters the wind and ultimately gives better protection than a solid 'wall' of trees.

Screens of trees can be useful within the garden as well as surrounding it. A popular choice for making light screens (and even hedges) is the Common Beech (*Fagus sylvatica*). Planted close together, about 1 m (3 ft 3 in) apart, they are then clipped to form a neat hedge. (It takes several years to grow a 1·2 m- [4 ft-] high hedge from container plants.) The leaves look good in both summer and autumn when they turn bronze-gold, but in winter only the branch structure remains, filtering the wind but not providing a solid screen. Hazels can also be trained to make a useful, dense hedge.

For screening patios and terraces, trees in containers are useful. Small standard trees like the bay (*Laurus nobilis*) provide quite solid evergreen cover. Among other possible tub trees are the tiny rowan, *Sorbus poteriifolia*, the miniature maple, *Acer palmatum* 'Corallinum' or glossy green *Ligustrum lucidum* (also in variegated forms).

For elegant dense screening, the yew (*Taxus baccata*) is unbeatable. It should be planted at intervals of about 1·5-1·75 m (5-6 ft). Eventually, after a good few years, it will make an elegant, thick, impenetrable hedge, ideal for screening a swimming pool, but patience is essential as the yew grows at the rate of only 15 cm (6 in) a year, and will need clipping to maintain a neat shape.

Trees can also be used very successfully in a town garden to screen off an ugly building that looms beyond its boundaries as well as to give more privacy. In a small garden, the best trees for this purpose are the fast-growing less spreading forms which will mask the unwanted view while not casting too much shade. A good choice might be a *Prunus* 'Amanogawa' and a birch (*Betula*), planted fairly close together.

LEFT *The sombre Purple Beech (*Fagus sylvatica *'Atropurpurea') forming the backcloth to this country cottage style scheme serves only to emphasize the freshness of the green, white and grey planting design and focuses attention on the centre of the garden.*

ABOVE *Pollarded plane trees (*Platanus orientalis*) have been used to protect a cliff top garden from the ravages of salt winds and sea gales. Because the trunks are dappled white their close formation is not oppressive.*

BELOW *Several trees, including the limes (*Tilia*) shown here, can be trained along poles or wires to form a light filtering screen. In this garden the formal rows have been imitated by clipped hedges of different heights to divide a large area into intimate enclosures.*

Avenues & Bowers

Since the very first gardens were created, trees have been used to provide shade and privacy. The pleasure they provide takes many forms, among them the dappled shade of foliage, the scented delights of blossom, the texture of the bark, or simply the enveloping effect of the branches at close quarters.

Creating bowers

In a small garden, a silver-leaved Willow Pear, *Pyrus salicifolia* 'Pendula', with a wooden bench below makes a perfect miniature natural bower; on a larger scale you can train a small avenue of flowering trees over a pergola or metal hoops.

The canopies of many of the large spreading trees make ideal natural bowers; it makes good sense to grasp the opportunity afforded by any such tree that you already have in your garden. You can add to its charm by growing a couple of outstanding specimens nearby: a *Malus floribunda* with its canopy of downy foliage and scented pink blossom, or the finely shaped leaves and fascinating marked bark of *Acer griseum* or the fragrant early flowers of *Magnolia salicifolia*. A few scented climbers, trained over existing trees, will add to the atmosphere: a vigorous 'Kiftsgate' rose perhaps, or one of the strongly perfumed honeysuckles, such as *Lonicera halliana*.

For a simple bower, seats or tables can be built or arranged around the trunk of a mature tree, under the shade of its spreading foliage – a bright-green-leaved *Ginkgo biloba* or a feathery-foliaged *Cedrela sinensis* are good subjects. In small gardens, you could use a quick-growing rowan, *Sorbus aucuparia* 'Beissneri' perhaps, which has yellow-green leaves and attractive orange bark. In fact any good-shaped tree that casts light dappled shade will serve, but avoid the heavy fruiting ones like mulberry, cherry, crab or plum because of the inconvenience of the dropping fruit. A mature weeping tree, like *Ilex aquifolium* 'Pendula' or *Fraxinus excelsior* 'Pendula', also makes a splendid bower.

The technique of creating a bower by training flowering or fruiting trees along wires or over hoops, to create a canopy of leaves and hanging blooms, is a throwback to the monastic gardens, where the bower or arbour provided fruit for the

RIGHT *Limes again, this time allowed to grow naturally and intertwined where the branches meet overhead to create a delightful shady path. Much of the pleasure of a lime avenue lies in the contrast between the fresh green foliage and the long slim dark trunks, but these are large trees and are really only suited to large-scale gardens.*

kitchen as well as a place for quiet contemplation. With fruit trees, you can plant two-year-old specimens which are then grafted together where their leaders meet. For a spectacular display of hanging blooms, the hybrid *Laburnum* × *watereri* 'Vossii' has particularly fine long drooping racemes of golden flowers.

A bower or arbour is good for sheltering and shading an exposed or too-sunny patio area. Light-foliaged trees like lime and linden (*Tilia*), the rich yellow *Robinia pseudacacia* 'Frisia', the hand-shaped leaves of the Japanese Maple (*Acer palmatum*) or the variegated Box Elder (*Acer negundo* 'Variegatum'), which is excellent for filtering sunshine, are all more natural and pleasing than a bright umbrella.

Remember that you may only need screening during the summer months, so choose a broad-leaved variety to prevent the area being too gloomy in winter. It is best to avoid trees with a heavy leaf drop that will smother the patio in the autumn months.

To create a temporary bower, standard trees can be grown in tubs and arranged close together.

Avenues and walks

Formal avenues of trees are mostly associated with the grand classical gardens of the past, but it is quite possible to recreate something similar on a much smaller scale. Specialist suppliers now offer a variety of tunnel shapes in good reproductions of classic styles, from simple constructions designed to cover a narrow pathway to altogether more elaborate versions up to 3 m (10 ft) wide and as long as you require. Laburnums, apples, pears or plums can be trained over them, and climbers like Clematis or Honeysuckle added for extra flowering interest. A path could be planted on either side

RIGHT *A single shady tree may provide the perfect place to put a table and chairs beneath its wide-spreading branches. You can create an instant bower with the bonus of glossy green foliage and sweet-scented flowers if you are lucky enough to own an ancient camellia like this one. Any type of spreading tree would do equally well.*

LEFT *A formal green avenue may be bordered by low clipped hedges, shaped evergreens, enormously tall dark cypress (*Cupressus sempervirens*) and pretty fruit trees – or a combination of all these as in this highly stylized French garden which uses a combination of different tree styles including orange, lemon and pomegranate trees. Note how trees are kept in check by low hedging or, in the case of the tall cypress, softened with smaller forms or species.*

with the Mountain Ash (*Sorbus* 'Joseph Rock'), whose delightful fern-like foliage is decorated with yellow berries in late summer and early autumn.

In a larger garden, you could create an informal walkway with a row of *Acer platanoides* 'Drummondii' or *Liriodendron tulipifera* 'Aureomarginata' – the variegated-leaved form of the Tulip Tree. For a more formal, elegant walkway, the Common Hornbeam (*Carpinus betulus*) can be clipped into box shapes or trained overhead to form a continuous canopy.

Other simple formal effects can be created using pairs of round-headed trees or trained evergreen standards such as bay (*Laurus nobilis*) or myrtle (*Myrtus luma*) either side of an entrance or to line a pathway like a guard of leafy sentinels.

BELOW *Here is another clever idea for a quick feature: in the middle of the lawn an old specimen tree with a good spreading habit makes a fine shady place to sit if you build a seat around the trunk or, in this case, trunks. Here a venerable cherry, so old that its stems are covered in green lichen, is given a new lease of life as a special kind of centrepiece.*

LEFT *Laburnum's generous display of buttery-yellow flowers makes it an ideal choice for training over hoops or overhead wires to form a flower-decked walkway. It makes a spectacular show, but need not be as large-scale as this: you could adapt the idea to a single arch or small pergola depending on the size of your garden. Laburnum is a fast grower but is not long-lived.*

Training & Clipping

Although every tree has its natural shape, from the narrow pyramid of some of the conifers to the generous spread of a crab apple or hawthorn, nature can be improved upon by trimming or training, both for practical and aesthetic reasons.

Topiary

The art of clipping trees into special shapes – topiary – has waxed and waned in popularity over the centuries, but has always been an integral part of formal garden design. Dense-foliaged evergreens like box, yew or privet make the ideal subjects and can be trimmed and trained into almost any shape that takes your fancy, from giant leafy lollipops to arches, spirals and even animal figures. Artificially shaped trees are not for low maintenance gardens or lazy gardeners. Unless you are prepared to spend the time maintaining the shape with regular clipping, you would be better advised to pick a tree with an interesting form and let nature do the work for you.

If you are very keen on having, say, a couple of clipped evergreens in pots, it is less difficult and time-consuming to maintain the shape once established than to create the shape for yourself. This entails regular clipping throughout the growing season as soon as each 5-10 cm (2-4 in) of growth has been made, to produce sufficiently dense leaves and the right close-textured effect.

Standards

A simpler form of shaping is to encourage a tree to form a standard – in other words to remove the lower branches from the main stem and allow the tree to form a mop-headed top, which can be

RIGHT *Pollarding stunts a tree's growth and encourages it to grow in a distorted shape. With this London Plane (*Platanus × acerifolia*), its new shape and mottled bark are well suited to its stony surroundings and yet it still provides welcome shade for an otherwise exposed courtyard. In this stark setting, the plane's bundles of light green leaves are a welcome breath of life and, like the bright yellow pansies in the raised bed, make a welcome splash of colour.*

LEFT *Not all clipped and shaped trees are tiny container specimens: these umbrella-headed* Prunus lusitanica *are large enough to partially shade a garden seat and have been planted in semi-raised enclosed beds alongside a wide pathway, making an excellent link between the formal and informal parts of the garden.*

clipped into a neat shape, such as a ball or pyramid. To induce the tree to achieve this shape you stake the tree to the eventual required height, lightly pinch out the side branches to within 15 cm (6 in) of the main stem and then pinch out the leading stem when the required height is reached. The lower branches are gradually removed as the top shoots are regularly but lightly pinched out, eventually creating a densely branched ball at the top of the tree and a clean, unbranched stem.

Training fruit trees

The other main reason for training trees is to produce a good crop from a fruit tree in a restricted space or to make harvesting easier. Espalier-, cordon- and fan-trained trees are an excellent way of producing fruit crops in small gardens or patios, and the two-dimensional, symmetrical effect is decorative as well as functional. They are best bought ready-trained so that only the very basic pruning is required.

An old-fashioned training device which is increasing in popularity is pegging, where fruiting branches are pegged down to the soil to produce interesting artificial weeping forms, most frequently used along formal borders (as in the gardens at Powis Castle in Wales).

Pleaching

Another attractive form of shaping is known as pleaching. A line of trees is allowed to grow to about 1.8 m (6 ft) or so before their tops are intertwined and then pruned to create an avenue or bower, or more simply a thick hedge. Quick-growing deciduous trees like lime and hornbeam are usually used. The branches are sometimes trained along wires to acquire the correct shape before they are clipped. In country districts, hedges of hawthorn (*Crataegus*), hazel (*Corylus avellana*) and other similar trees are often pleached or laid, so that the growth is sideways rather than upwards, creating a more impenetrable hedge.

To avoid damage to the branches while training trees the best practice is to fix canes to the wires and attach the branches to them loosely with ties or twine for support.

LEFT *A fan-trained or espalier fruit tree against a sunny wall not only makes an attractive two-dimensional feature and interesting wall cover, but also enables you to grow fruit in a limited space where you might not otherwise have room for a full-scale fruit tree. This espalier pear makes an excellent decorative feature too with its fine spring blossom.*

LEFT *The close-foliaged Hornbeam (*Carpinus betulus*) is another tree which may be trained and intertwined to form leafy archways and walkways. The stems are tall and straight and the round heads easily clipped into curves and domes. Hardy and easy to grow, the Hornbeam is deciduous so is well suited for shading areas which need protection from sun in summer but plenty of light in winter. Below, the small golden Lawson's Cypress (*Chamaecyparis lawsoniana *'Lutea') adds bright highlights.*

ABOVE *Not quite formal enough to be called an avenue, yet too regular to be classed as woodland despite a carpet of spring bulbs below, this row of lime trees (*Tilia*), with its light trunks and fresh green foliage stands out against a dark surrounding hedge of Yew (*Taxus baccata*).*

Oriental Effects

In a Japanese garden you are immediately aware of the visual excitement of trees throughout the seasons, for shape and scale, bark texture, special weeping or contorted forms and, most importantly, colour, are all exploited to achieve the desired effect. Trees may be grouped to create a small natural woodland area or used alone as a focal point like that jewel of the Japanese garden, the Japanese Maple (*Acer palmatum*). With its full-bodied, uplifted outline of foliage and spectacular colour in summer and autumn, even the individual leaves are a garden designer's dream: delicately hand-shaped and changing from fresh lime-green to a wonderful deep crimson.

Trees like the Japanese Maple look at their best among other architectural elements of Japanese garden design: hummocks and carpets of green moss, a pool of pebbles, low ground-covering plants, bamboos and water – essential for reflecting branches and sky, for adding light and movement especially in the *kare sansui* or dry landscape garden created from stones and rock. These natural elements are combined to construct the impression of mountains, hills, lakes and groves.

The correct balance of scale, shape and colour is crucial in such a scheme and trees must be carefully chosen to achieve the right effect without upsetting the balance of nature. This is the real skill of the designer of a Japanese garden, where every part can be enjoyed as much as the whole.

Of all gardeners and landscapers, it is the Japanese who have really grasped the importance and design potential of trees. 'There are no particular rules for constructing a garden,' wrote Li Chi-cheng in the 16th century, 'but for the borrowing of landscapes there are certain techniques, and they are of the greatest importance in designing a garden with trees.'

Shakkei, literally 'borrowed landscape', is the grandest and most ambitious style of Japanese garden design, where a distant view of mountains, a waterfall, maybe a valley or even a sacred temple, is subtly incorporated into the general scheme. The trunks of tall trees like the red or black pine may be used to frame it, or a variety of trees planned on different levels to create a woodland 'stroll garden', one you may wander around on a system of winding paths and enjoy in every season. Every tree, plant and man-made addition to the garden is designed not to distract and should lead the eye naturally towards the view beyond.

Completely different are the familiar and finely tuned Japanese courtyard gardens, developed from the traditional tea garden or *tsubonouchi*. Here the essential design elements can be traced back to their original intention: the stepping stones across thick moss, water or pebbles leading

RIGHT *The essential element of an oriental garden – the Japanese Maple (*Acer palmatum *'Atropurpureum'), which comes in a wide choice of sizes, shapes and colours to suit every season and all tastes. It is prized mainly for its beautiful foliage which may be deeply cut like this specimen, often turning into a fabulous kaleidoscope of colour in autumn. This small hybrid with snake-like stems is set off by other traditional elements of Japanese garden design: the mosses, boulders and methodically raked sand.*

RIGHT *A strong background of evergreens is highlighted at certain times of the year by brilliant flashes of pure colour, often sited beside an informal pool where the water's reflection heightens its impact. This may take the form of a decorative Japanese maple turning scarlet or bronze in autumn; or, in spring, that of the breath-taking flowers of an azalea or rhododendron.*

the guest at a leisured pace to the *Nijiri guchi* or door of the tea-house; the stone lantern designed to light the garden for night-time ceremonies and the stone basin for the ritual washing of hands. Water, stone and restrained planting is intended to be enjoyed from within the garden, to create a pleasant and contemplative approach to the tea-house, never a view from it. It is an enclosed and tranquil style that has been eagerly adopted in today's town gardens. Traditionally trees tended to be incorporated as a single decorative specimen in the tea garden: a handsome willow, plum or maple. This inclusion of the tree purely as an element of design was a bold and single-minded statement of the garden designer, for a single tree was generally considered unlucky.

Japanese gardening techniques were not analysed until the early 20th century; by then the basic principles had been honed and refined into an exacting and disciplined format which had nevertheless lost none of its affinity with nature. Thus sky, rock, water – and trees – are essential elements even in the smallest gardens where clipped forms and bonsai were developed to maintain the correct scale.

BELOW *The simplest elements may conjure up a Japanese feel in a small patio garden: bamboo screening, dark green ground cover and climbers, a small* Pinus parviflora *'Glauca' and the tiniest water feature – an attractive stone bowl.*

BELOW *The Japanese in particular prize trees that have delicate leaf shapes and interesting colouring, like* Sorbus, *which needs only an arrangement of mossy boulders to show off its superb autumn tints.*

LEFT *Other trees are naturally small enough to be grown in tubs or containers. The tiny Japanese Maple (*Acer palmatum *'Dissectum') looks best in a low bowl or Chinese-style urn to enhance its exotic shape and appearance. It usually stands alone as a specimen tree, but the container should be softened with boulders and clumps of bright green moss. This small town garden has reinforced its oriental theme with water, large rocks, gravel and a temple ornament. Tall evergreens (* × Cupressocyparis*) all round provide the necessary privacy and seclusion, peace and tranquillity.*

Trees in Miniature

If correctly grown and carefully displayed, bonsai trees can be used to create a fascinating world in miniature. Employing the technique – the raising, pruning, feeding and watering of trees in small containers – is in itself enjoyable if you have the patience, and the result is wholly satisfying.

The art of bonsai

The Japanese, who developed the art of tree miniaturization and who gave it its name (bonsai means 'plant in a tray'), use bonsai not only as a decorative detail or to demonstrate their skills with plants, but also as a way to observe and enjoy nature at close hand. The trees are sometimes mistakenly kept indoors and there is great disappointment when they begin to die off. Bonsai trees are still trees and have all the same climatic requirements as the parent, with good shelter as well in deference to their tiny size.

A bonsai arrangement is ideally positioned on the patio or within a small courtyard plan, raised up on wooden stands, on a table top or set into a niche to bring it closer to eye level. The trees are usually planted in special glazed ceramic trays or pots which are available both from garden centres and independent potteries. They are deliberately shallow – correctly no more than a half to one third the size of the upper part of the tree so that it can be easily seen and the roots can develop without becoming too extensive. The size of the container must always be in proportion to the tree (or trees) and its colour harmonious. From a practical point of view, the containers must have drainage holes for good air circulation; small feet to raise them off the surface also helps in this respect; and often they have matching drip-trays.

Choosing bonsai trees

Originally, trees were collected from mountain and coastal regions where they had been naturally stunted and miniaturized, but such collection is no longer acceptable. For a specimen tree, choose a type with outstanding features like a Japanese Maple (*Acer palmatum*) or Twisted Pine (*Pinus contorta*), combined with gravel, mosses and large stones to reproduce a natural landscape. For larger trays, several trees of a single species may be

BELOW *A gnarled trunk and mature, slightly windswept shape deserves to be displayed alone without the distractions of other trees or even a fancy trough. This* Podocarpus macrophyllus *is only enhanced by the tiny figure sitting on the rocks at its feet, obviously lost in contemplation.*

RIGHT *A collection of bonsai trees can be displayed together on a special raised area such as this old mill wheel or on a timber platform which allows their tiny form to be more easily appreciated. Here dwarfed and bonsai forms have been carefully arranged in a variety of pots and troughs, which, although they are in different shapes and sizes, are still complementary in colour and texture.*

grown to create miniature groves or woodlands of pine, beech, birch or larch.

Evergreens, particularly pine, juniper and spruce, are popular subjects; short-needled types are best here from the point of view of scale and the growing tip has to be pinched out (never cut), sometimes daily, during the growing season. Especially prized for bonsai are the Japanese Black Pine (*Pinus thunbergii*), the Japanese Cryptomeria (*Cryptomeria japonica*) and the Chinese Juniper (*Juniperus chinensis*). However, deciduous species with interesting foliage and good autumn colour can be worth a tray of bare twigs through winter; the Japanese are particularly fond of *Acer trifidum*, birch (*Betula*) and hornbeam (*Carpinus*). Selected shoots are removed to produce a mature-looking tree after four to five years, although bonsai trees can live for hundreds of years, producing spectacular miniature bark effects and gnarled forms. Fruiting and flowering trees must be chosen carefully for while the leaves and branches can be dwarfed, these features will remain close to their natural size. Select species with naturally smaller fruits or blossom like cotoneaster or crab apple (*Malus*).

To prematurely age them and create interesting shapes and forms, the trees are usually trained using wires and clips, making them look windswept, distorted or gnarled. Some are even grown with their roots exposed, clinging to a piece of rock to simulate a cliff. Groups look best in uneven numbers, sometimes raised on a small mound, or in the case of conifers, layered to create a grove effect.

Bonsai need patience to train and conscientious maintenance. They must be watered with rainwater whenever dry – this could be twice a day in summer, preferably in the early morning or evening – and they should also be given fertilizer frequently in spring and summer. More detailed information on caring for bonsai trees is given on page 181.

Pots & Containers

Although trees are not the first subjects perhaps that spring to mind as being suitable for growing in tubs and pots, there are many species which are: not just the familiar evergreens like Bay (*Laurus nobilis*) or Box (*Buxus sempervirens*), but hollies, Japanese maples and fig trees. Trees in containers make an excellent, practical feature on the patio, terrace or roof garden. Containers will naturally restrict their size, bringing them down to a suitable scale and making them easier to manage, yet their height is useful for screening or shelter and their foliage makes excellent natural shade or an area of special interest above shrubs and smaller tub plants. You may also have the opportunity to grow trees with very specific soil requirements that perhaps would not flourish in the rest of the garden: a lime-hater like *Camellia,* for example, or an acid-loving *Rhododendron.* You could also experiment with more tender varieties, like citrus fruit trees (orange tend to be tougher than lemon), which will enjoy a sunny sheltered patio in summer and can be brought indoors in winter. Many gardeners these days are experimenting successfully with exotic fruit trees.

Containers must be plenty large enough to take the root growth and to ensure the trees are stable, but if you position the pots on low wooden platforms with castors attached they are still completely portable, and can be moved to a key position as the seasons change to focus attention on, say, a flowering variety at its peak.

Small-leaved trees like laurel, box, yew and privet can be clipped into attractive geometric or ornamental shapes and are good subjects (although difficult to match) for pairing up in matching tubs or urns to stand either side of a doorway or for planting in stone or timber troughs to make a continuous hedge. These formal shapes look good around a pool, a hot tub or seating area, yet can be removed in winter or repositioned to enclose new areas as required.

Dwarf conifers are small and slow growing, and make ideal container subjects. Combined with ivies, heather and low-growing shrubs like juniper, they can be used to create miniature woodland effects or soft moulded contours of different shapes and colours can be used to hide an unsightly part of the garden. The height provided by the tub and the close proximity of other plants creates much more impact than dotting them around the main garden. *Chamaecyparis* is a good subject here – maybe *C. thyoides* or the deep green upright *C. lawsoniana* 'Ellwoodii'. Take full advantage of the different colour varieties available from the blue-grey pillar of *C.l.* 'Columnaris' to the tiny gold *C.l.* 'Minima Aurea' to provide a backbone for your tub planting.

Other trees worth growing in containers for their interesting foliage include many of the

LEFT *Dark green box trees, when clipped into tiny domes and lollipops, are the perfect foil for natural terracotta pots. Use them as ornaments on the patio in groups or in pairs to disguise its shape or to liven up a dull corner. In this very small backyard, Japanese box trees (* Buxus microphylla*) are particularly appropriate against russet brick paving and an evergreen screen of ivy to maintain a simple two-colour scheme.*

ABOVE RIGHT *You can use small trees in containers to soften structural features. In this tiny oriental garden the unusual foliage of* Acer palmatum *'Atropurpureum' is perfectly positioned in a large Chinese urn topped with pebbles and surrounded by the sculptural mound-forming greenery of* Helxine soleirolii.

hollies (*Ilex*), some of which have variegated leaves; the smaller Japanese maples (*Acer palmatum*) and, for an exotic or oriental setting, a relatively hardy palm like the Chinese Fan Palm (*Trachycarpus fortunei*). These are all useful for making a natural focal point and are large enough to hold the attention with a spectacular display, but not so huge that they dominate the planting or produce too much shade. *Camellia japonica* is a fine flowering container tree for shady corners.

Plant your trees in inexpensive wooden barrels, large frost-resistant terracotta pots or even glazed Chinese urns for exotic species. Remember to raise the pots off the ground to prevent ice forming and cracking them. If not frost-proof they will have to be brought under cover in colder weather. Bare soil on top means faster water evaporation, so cover it with pebbles or plant spring bulbs like crocus, snowdrops and narcissi around them.

If you follow the design principles outlined on pages 10-14 you will produce the most satisfactory arrangement of container trees. Just as important, though, is the fact that trees in tubs need particular care and require diligent (daily in summer) feeding and watering if they are to survive and flourish (see page 180).

CLIMBERS IN TREES

TRAILING ONE or two climbing plants through a tree can provide useful colour when the tree itself is not making much of a display. This is ideal for a small garden; for creating visual tricks, like a sweet-scented 'honeysuckle tree' overhanging the patio (try *Lonicera japonica*); or for breathing new life into an old tree, worth keeping for its size and shape. A breathtaking spring blanket of *Clematis montana*, with long grass and bulbs or wild flowers below, looks delightful and a variegated hybrid ivy like *Hedera helix* 'Goldheart' makes a stunning show of brightness most of the year

Climbers can be used with more valued, flourishing trees too, provided the tree is well established so that the climber is not competing with it for moisture and nourishment. It need not be planted directly below the host tree although some, like clematis and honeysuckle, enjoy having their roots in shade and their flowers in the light.

Climbers trained along branches or across wires to link trees create an unusual walkway or pergola. A vigorous climbing rose like the white-flowered *Rosa filipes* 'Kiftsgate' or the superb *Wisteria sinensis* with its pendulous lilac (or white) clusters of flowers makes a wonderful fragrant roof. As well as creating arches, pergolas and walkways, trees may be linked with climbers to other, architectural features such as trellis or buildings, perhaps to provide interest above eye level or make useful shelter. Or choose two climbing rose varieties to bloom in succession after your tree's own blossom has finished – a useful trick for an early-blooming variety of *Prunus* or *Malus*.

Annual climbers are also useful as short-lived but fast-growing cover-ups and are an excellent way to ring the changes in your garden scheme. One year it might be purple-flowered Morning Glory (*Ipomoea*); another, a multi-coloured display of scented sweet peas (*Lathyrus*) or the pretty Japanese Hop (*Humulus japonicus*). Fruiting climbers add a sybaritic touch to a sunny garden: dessert grapes like *Vitis* 'Black Hamburg' are an obvious choice; more unusual would be the Chinese Gooseberry or Kiwi Fruit (*Actinidia chinensis*) which is worth growing for its pretty foliage alone, even if you don't have the kind of climate that will encourage it to make fruit.

BELOW *Clematis is a popular climber for covering all manner of objects in the garden from trees, trellis and pergolas to an eyesore that needs a quick disguise. However, this* Clematis × *'Jackmanii' has not been planted to do an effective cover-up job, but chosen rather to enhance the tree's own golden foliage with its startling contrast of deep purple colour. The tree is an* Ulmus procera *'Louis van Houtte' with a narrow upright habit allowing it to squeeze into the smallest of patios.*

LEFT *A prolific climber,* Rosa *'Wedding Day' scrambles over an informal arch and up into an old apple tree to make a special summer feature and a delightful flowering gateway leading from one part of the garden to another. It would be possible to train a later variety over the same area to provide an extended season of blooms.*

UNDERPLANTING TREES

A TREE RISING out of billowing, luxuriant foliage, or long grass spangled with wild flowers or spring bulbs, is so much more appealing than one standing forlornly in a bare patch of earth. Giving proper thought to the area around and beneath your tree (or trees) will help to integrate it with the rest of your garden scheme. But equally a small sea of leaf shapes and colours could be used to isolate a specimen tree on its own 'island'; or pebbles, stones or bark chips used as cover where the area is too shady for plants to grow as a means of minimizing water evaporation from tree roots (particularly important where trees are grown in containers). (Beware in hot climates of the glare from stones damaging the stems of the trees.) On sloping sites, groundcover plants help bind and stabilize the soil.

Your chosen plants must be shade-tolerant. Some trees have a denser canopy than others and the ground is drier because rain will not easily penetrate; very little at all will then grow under them. Conifers – their needle drop makes the soil extremely acidic in any case – are an example and some trees, like Horse Chestnut (*Aesculus*), grow almost down to the ground.

Underplanting with shrubs

Shrubs make the ideal 'step down' from trees in height, provided they are compatible. Some of the bigger flowering shrubs like rhododendron and azalea may be unsuitable for planting close to shallow-rooted trees such as birch and ash but do well under oaks and pines. Some, like *Daphne mezereum*, can offer the bonus of scented flowers in winter; others like *Hypericum* and *Juniperus* are low-growing with plenty of colour and shape variety for all seasons. The evergreen bramble *Rubus tricolor* has glossy green leaves and is ideal

LEFT *No-one could miss this* Magnolia × soulangiana *enclosed by a low hedge of clipped box (* Buxus sempervirens*) and rising majestically in full flower out of a billowing mass of* Rodgersia *with its giant-sized lobed leaves – one of the most dramatic ground-cover plants. It does not mind the dappled shade provided by the Magnolia and could not provide a better contrast with the tiny evergreen leaves of the Box.*

RIGHT Genista aetnensis *is extravagant with its huge spread of branches dripping green and yellow and its heady fragrance, but it is not greedy for light and space. Its delicate form produces only the lightest of shade, allowing a wide range of flowering plants including border perennials, to be grown under its feathery canopy.*

for banks and steep slopes; or choose something with variegated leaves to brighten up a dark corner: the spotted Laurel (*Aucuba japonica crotonoides*) or holly (*Ilex aquifolium*) are ideal but some variegated plants tend to lose their markings when grown in shade.

Underplanting with ground cover

Vigorous spreading plants or low-growing ramblers will quickly cover any bare patches and bring your scheme neatly down to ground level. *Vinca major* or *V. minor* and one or two of the many interesting ivy hybrids make excellent cover; any woodland plant like *Pulmonaria angustifolia* and *Convallaria major* (Lily-of-the-Valley) should do well in moist soil and dappled shade.

Try to get a good range of foliage shape and colour: a grass like *Luzulus* or *Carex* may be all you can grow in deep shade but is useful for its spiky blades. For lighter shade and moist conditions, the large quilted leaves of *Hosta* are real eyecatchers, as are giant peltiphyllums with foliage like large parasols and the flowering *Rodgersia pinnata* which has deeply cut foliage.

A damp and shady situation is the obvious place to grow ferns whose lush exotic foliage is such a perfect foil for trees. Many require a rich soil and most enjoy dappled light rather than dense shade. Most spectacular perhaps is the Royal Fern (*Osmunda regalis*) with its wonderful bronze autumn colour; others with unusual shapes are the compact but rather tender Bird's Nest Fern (*Asplenium nidus*) and the Hart's Tongue Fern (*Phyllitis scolopendrium*) which makes a head of crinkled fronds and which is reasonably hardy.

Coping with dry shade

In the hot, dry garden, underplanting may be difficult where shade is dense. There are several drought-loving grass-type plants such as *Liriope*

LEFT *Where trees are planted on a slope or incline, permanent ground cover of small shrubs and vigorous perennials helps to bind the soil together and prevent erosion, as well as creating an excellent vertical display. This large area is particularly well planted with a wide variety of leaf shapes and a pleasing mixture of golds, greys and greens which look wonderful against the dark trunks of the young oak trees.*

FAR LEFT *The wide-spreading umbrella of trailing blooms produced by* Prunus × yedoensis *'Ivensii' is so showy, and the leaf canopy later produces a fairly dense shade, making the choice of ground-cover plants difficult. Here deep green ground-covering* Cotoneaster *and the soft pink flowers and shiny green leaves of a large clump of shade-tolerant* Bergenia *are companionable without competing for attention.*

muscari and *Ophiopogon japonicum* (Japanese Mondo Grass) which looks good with stones or pebbles. For the oriental-style garden choose the spiky dwarf bamboos – the *Sasa* species make good vigorous ground cover. You may find most of the best-growing ground-cover plants too invasive and this goes for the quick-spreading buttercup *Ranunculus repens*, so perfect for an instant informal scheme. *R. bulbosa* 'Flore Plena', which produces no seed, is less rampant.

Some flowering plants like *Tiarella cordifolia* will tolerate shady or semi-shade conditions. Generally though, for most of the year, you will have to rely on the cool white flowers of many of the shade-loving plants to brighten dark areas. *Allium ursinum* (Wild Garlic) has white flowers in late spring and a pungent scent.

The areas under trees can come into their own in spring with flowering bulbs like snowdrops, narcissi, aconites and erythroniums among the grass beneath deciduous trees; or for a woodland flavour, persevere with some of the native flowering plants such as periwinkle, cyclamen, woodruff and, for light dappled shade, foxgloves.

LEFT *Dappled light from the tree canopy makes a useful habitat for shade-loving plants. Here, ferns, hellebores and ivies carpet a woodland dell (in my own garden – AP). Trees are kept under control, pruned just enough to allow light through to encourage the planting on the woodland floor to look lush and verdant.*

RIGHT *On the edge of a wood or where the light shade from trees protects the soil below from drying winds, large-leaved moisture-loving plants will usually survive. Here* Petasites japonicus, Petasites alba, Ligularia dentata *'Desdemona' in flower and the invasive* Impatiens roylei *border a shady path (again in my garden – AP).*

Edible Fruits

Trees producing edible fruits, nuts and berries surely offer the best of all possible worlds. For as well as the visual pleasure of those glossy colours among the foliage and the fine display of blossom in spring, there is the satisfaction of eating one's own produce picked straight from the tree. Indeed these are the fruits of minimum labour: you may only have to spray against insects and prune the odd dead branch to obtain a good crop.

You should make sure when choosing fruit trees to pick a dessert cultivar with a good flavour as today not all fruit tree varieties have been developed for their flavour or edibility. Many varieties are more disease-resistant, fruit earlier (although be prepared to wait a couple of years at least) and are smaller than formerly, without any reduction in crop yields.

A fruit tree needs room to develop properly and should be kept away from any paved areas where dropping fruit or bird lime would create a messy nuisance. If you are short of space, try one of the two-dimensional fan or cordon types against a wall or fence. The Morello Cherry (*Prunus cerasus* 'Austera'), for example, will grow against a north-facing wall (where little else can) and makes a delicious jam or liqueur.

Where you only have room for one tree, your favourite may make an excellent specimen tree if, like the Black Mulberry (*Morus nigra*), it has an attractive spreading habit and plenty of interest through the seasons. Larger gardens might have room for a group of three or five fruit trees: maybe three apples, a plum and a pear. Try to plant a selection of different varieties, perhaps by

using 'family' trees, with three or five different varieties grafted onto one rootstock.

In a Mediterranean or subtropical climate a citrus grove may be appropriate. Because it often takes more than a single year for oranges and lemons to ripen, you can enjoy fruit, flowers and foliage simultaneously. Depending on climate, you can experiment with other exotic fruits either outside or behind glass in an unheated lean-to against a sunny wall. The luscious late-summer fruiting Fig (*Ficus carica*) is quite hardy and best grown in a tub or pot where its roots are restricted. It needs heavy pruning, but beware of the milky sap which is highly irritant.

There are other fine trees you can plant in the garden that will satisfy both gourmet and gardener. Trees with edible berries or fruits like the Rowan (*Sorbus*), Crab Apple (*Malus*) or Quince (*Cydonia oblonga*) have excellent blossom and foliage interest and are well suited to a wild or country-style garden. None of them makes a large tree and their bright fruits and berries in late summer have the added bonus that they can be made into delicious jellies and conserves.

Nor should the trees that have edible nuts be forgotten: the Walnut (*Juglans regia*) is a handsome if slow-growing tree for warmer areas and most gardens have room for a small hazelnut or cobnut (*Corylus avellana*) or almond (*Prunus dulcis*) with its sweet-scented blossom. Less common but no less appealing is the Medlar (*Mespilus germanica*); the fruits make a good jelly or pickle.

LEFT *The Citrus Orange is an attractive small tree and in a warm climate will bear plenty of fruit, remaining on the tree for two years so that you can enjoy both flowers and fruit at the same time. Quite apart from the fact that the fruits are edible, this makes a fine decorative specimen with its glossy green leaves and glowing orange fruits. If the winter is too severe, grow the orange trees in pots and bring them indoors at the end of summer.*

RIGHT *Fan-training and espalier techniques may be ancient crafts but in today's much smaller gardens are an excellent means of growing fruit in a small space. Even a north-facing wall can be utilized by growing a Morello Cherry, delicious for jam and with the bonus of a superb display of blossom in spring.*

FAR LEFT *You cannot beat an apple tree for its small but spreading shape, sweet-scented spring blossom and delicious fruit.*

—IV—

A GUIDE TO GARDEN TREES

There are some trees that are undoubtedly more garden worthy than others, either because they have a succession of attractive features over several seasons, or because they have particularly handsome features. In this chapter, the trees most suitable for gardens (and in particular small- or medium-sized gardens) have been selected. The first part of the chapter takes the larger groups like flowering cherries (*Prunus*), and crab apples (*Malus*), and lists some of the best species and cultivars, complete with information on height, speed of growth and hardiness as well as their botanical descriptions and specific cultivation needs. Then in an A-Z section we have selected more than 350 trees that are especially suitable for gardens. In each case the eventual height the tree will make (although this will vary according to the prevailing conditions) has been given, as well as an approximate idea of its speed of growth – S, M or F indicates slow-, medium- or fast-growing respectively. The zonal rating (Z) at the beginning of each entry indicates the hardiness of the tree (see page 192 for a key to zonal information).

Mixed planting of Pinus sylvestris, Larix decidua *and* Tsuga heterophylla

Acer

Widely used as ornamental trees in Japanese-style gardens, the maples have several outstanding features which make them an excellent choice for almost any type of garden. They come in a wide range of shapes and sizes, many of them admittedly too large for most gardens, but there is still a fine selection of much smaller species and cultivars, many of which grow to only about 6 m (20 ft).

Acers can easily be identified by their typical palmate (hand-shaped) leaves which vary from the wide, spreading fingers of the Norway Maple (*A. platanoides*) to the delightful finely cut lace-like foliage of one of the Japanese maples, *A. palmatum* 'Dissectum'. Maples are often good value in town gardens, as many are pollution-tolerant and their delicate, richly coloured foliage makes a welcome diversion in grey city streets. The flowers of many maples are insignificant but the range and beauty of the leaves is so great that this hardly matters. They offer singularly attractive autumn colour in shades from gold to deep scarlet and crimson.

The needs of maples vary according to type, but many are fairly tolerant. They all need space to spread themselves so that their form and foliage can be properly appreciated.

RIGHT *(main picture) With its glorious autumn colour and delicately cut leaves,* Acer palmatum *'Dissectum' is one of the most attractive Japanese maples. Small enough to be grown in a border, it is still handsome enough to stand alone as a specimen tree, if required.*

INSET *(right) This venerable* Acer palmatum *'Dissectum Purpureum', grown as a standard, makes an eye-catching focal point at a curve in a path. Planting it against a contrasting background of fresh green foliage, as has been done here, serves to emphasize both its handsome form and striking foliage colour.*

INSET *(far right)* Acer palmatum heptalobum *is a small tree with a spreading habit and a dense mass of foliage that turns gold and bronze at the end of the year.*

Acer palmatum JAPANESE MAPLE
Z: 5 H: 6 m (20 ft) S–M
This group is undoubtedly the most beautiful and the most garden-worthy of all the maples, particularly for small gardens. Japanese maples are all slow growing, rarely to more than about 6 m (20 ft) in cultivation, although they are often considerably larger in the wild. They have been developed to produce many different forms with minor variations of leaf type and colour.

They are tolerant of shade, but do best in a sunny position in good soil. They are often susceptible to late frosts and to cold, drying winds.

The following are hardy to zone 5.

***A.p.* 'Atropurpureum'**
Rich red leaves.

***A.p.* 'Aureum'**
Yellow-leaved, turning golden later.

***A.p.* 'Dissectum'**
A very small tree, 3 m (10 ft) at most, that is ideal for borders and as a specimen tree. It has delicately cut, lace-like foliage. A purple-leaved form, ***A.p.* 'Dissectum Atropurpureum',** is also very attractive.

A.p. heptalobum
Found wild in Japan, this tree has larger leaves than *A. palmatum*, each with seven lobes.

***A.p.* 'Osakazuki'**
Said to be the best maple for brilliant scarlet and orange autumn colour.

***A.p.* 'Senkaki'** (*A.p.* 'Sango Kaku')
CORAL BARK MAPLE
Beautiful coral-red stems that look good in winter and prettily cut light-green leaves that turn yellowish-orange in autumn. It eventually grows to about 7 m (25 ft).

OTHER MAPLES

A. campestre HEDGE or FIELD MAPLE
Z: 5 H: 7·5 m (25 ft) S
A good screen tree, with yellow autumn colour.

A. cappadocicum CAUCASIAN MAPLE
Z: 6 H: 20 m (65 ft) M
Needs plenty of space. Glossy green

medium-sized leaves, attractive yellow autumn colour. Yellow flowers in spring. ***A.c.* 'Rubrum'** A good garden cultivar, with blackish-red leaves.

A. circinatum VINE MAPLE
Z: 3 H: 6 m (20 ft) S
One of the few small maples with both ornamental flowers and good autumn colouring.

A. griseum PAPERBARK MAPLE
Z: 6 H: 9 m (30 ft) S
Notable peeling bark. Good red autumn colour.

A. japonicum FULL MOON MAPLE
Z: 5 H: 9 m (30 ft) M
Small bushy tree with red flowers and bright red autumn colour. ***A.j.* 'Viti-folium'** Striking autumn colours.

A. negundo BOX ELDER
Z: 3 H: 20 m (65 ft) F
Very tough tree with bright green leaves. Makes a good screening tree, and thrives in poor soil. There are silver, cream or yellow variegated forms.

A. platanoides NORWAY MAPLE
Z: 4 H: 30 m (100 ft) S
Prominent yellow flower clusters in spring and strong yellow autumn colour. Tolerant of salt and pollution. There are several cultivars with a more compact habit, including ***A.p.* 'Drummondii'** with variegated foliage.

A. pseudoplatanus SYCAMORE MAPLE
Z: 5 H: 30 m (100 ft) F
Good shade-casting tree with dark green summer foliage and yellow flowers in spring. Tolerant of most soils. Some smaller cultivars available including ***A.p.* 'Brilliantissimum'** which has pink and, later, fresh lime-green foliage and ***A.p.* 'Worleei'** with golden foliage.

A. rubrum RED MAPLE
Z: 3 H: 36 m (120 ft) M
Red flowers on red branches in early spring. Does not thrive on chalk.

ABOVE *A small formal walkway has been lined with matched pairs of* Acer pseudoplatanus *'Brilliant-issimum' seen here in juvenile form. The foliage when it first appears is tinged with pink, turning golden later in the season.*

LEFT *The Caucasian Maple (*Acer cappadocicum*) needs plenty of space to spread itself and to show off its excellent golden autumn foliage colour in all its glory.*

LEFT *The Red Maple (*Acer rubrum*) is distinguished not only by rich scarlet autumn foliage but also by its small red flowers in early spring, followed by bright red clusters of keys. With something to offer in every season, it is a valuable tree for the garden.*

FAR LEFT *Grown mainly for its round-headed shape and pleasant bright green leaves, the Norway Maple (*Acer platanoides*) also offers good yellow autumn colour. The cultivar shown here,* A.p. *'Drummondii', is the form normally grown in gardens.*

AESCULUS

THE DECIDUOUS horsechestnuts and buckeyes that comprise the genus *Aesculus* are instantly recognizable by their handsome spreading bulk and strong, dark trunks. If space is limited, the smaller varieties can be grown like the Red Buckeye (*A. pavia*) and the Californian Buckeye (*A. californica*).

In late spring and early summer they hold aloft a mass of upright spikes or 'candles' of flowers. Even the early leaf buds are attractive – large and glistening brown. In summer the trees are a solid mass of large dense green hand-shaped leaves offering valuable shade. Not all species have good autumn colour, but *A. flava* or *A. turbinata* are excellent in this respect.

BELOW *The easily identifiable large-lobed leaves of the Common Horse Chestnut (*Aesculus hippocastanum*) turn a good colour in autumn. The Horse Chestnut is seen at its best as a centrepiece in a large lawn.*

RIGHT *The Red Horse Chestnut (*Aesculus × carnea*). In early summer the bright pink candles of flowers light up the tree but the foliage does not colour well in autumn. (Inset)* A. × c. *'Briotii' – a smaller form with red flowers.*

A. californica CALIFORNIAN BUCKEYE
Z: 5 H: 10·5 m (35 ft) S
Good choice for a small garden. The summer flower spikes are pink/white and fragrant.

A.* × *carnea RED HORSECHESTNUT
Z: 6 H: 21·5 m (70 ft) M
Red/pink flower spikes. ***A.* × *c.* 'Briotii'** is a small cultivar with tall spikes of red flowers.

A.* × *flava SWEET BUCKEYE
Z: 5 H: 27·5 m (90 ft) M
Yellow flower spikes in early summer. Good autumn colour.

A. hippocastanum COMMON HORSECHESTNUT
Z: 5 H: 36 m (120 ft) F
Popular shade tree. White flower 'candles'. ***A.h.* 'Baumanni'** has double flowers and no conkers. ***A.h.* 'Pyramidalis'** forms a neat fastigiate shape.

A. indica INDIAN HORSECHESTNUT
Z: 7 H: 27 m (85 ft) M
A tree worth considering for its combination of large shiny buds, dark green leaves opening with a bronze colour, pink/white flower spikes and unusual shiny black conkers.

A. neglecta 'Erythroblastos'
Z: 5 H: 30 m (100 ft) S
Tender but worth growing for the early foliage which is pale pinky cream, turning lime-green later.

A. × parviflora
Z: 5 H: 6 m (20 ft) S
Small neat shrubby tree with spikes of white flowers in mid- to late summer.

A. pavia RED BUCKEYE
Z: 5 H: 6 m (20 ft) S
A good small tree with deep crimson flowers.

BELOW *The Sweet Buckeye (*Aesculus × flava*) with its good autumn colour and distinctive shape makes a useful tree for larger gardens. The early summer flowers are yellow.*

BETULA

SLENDER, delicate and often fast-growing, birches look their best set in graceful groups against a background of dark evergreens to show off their pale stems and light foliage. Tall silver- and grey-stemmed species are useful for lightening up dark areas; those with peeling or orange bark offer excellent winter interest.

Birches may grow to 6 m (20 ft) in as short a time as ten years or less and although most young trees have plain brown trunks, they will produce a variety of interesting bark effects and colours, according to type, as they mature. Silver- and grey-barked varieties have wide-spreading roots so they should be planted well away from walls and foundations. The early foliage is a very attractive pale green, turning brighter green in summer and then usually golden-yellow by autumn. Birches produce fine catkins, both male and female, which contribute to the 'weeping' effect. They are hardy trees, enjoying full sun, but they are prone to quite a few diseases and to insect damage.

B. albo-sinensis
Z: 4 H: 23 m (75 ft) M
Orange-red bark with coppery sheen.

B. lutea YELLOW BIRCH
Z: 2 H: up to 30 m (100 ft) – depending on climate M
Dull green leaves and golden bark.

B. nigra RIVER BIRCH
Z: 4 H: 27 m (90 ft) F
Makes a pyramidal shape and has dramatic black and white peeling bark. Good in damp locations.

B. papyrifera PAPER BIRCH, CANOE BIRCH
Z: 4 H: 21·5 m (70 ft) F
Very white trunks with attractive, peeling, papery bark.

B. pendula COMMON SILVER BIRCH
Z: 2 H: 12-21·5 m (40-70 ft) F
A short-lived tree with white bark and single or multiple trunks. The following are just some of the many cultivars of *B. pendula*.

***B.p.* 'Dalecarlica'** Also known as SWEDISH BIRCH. Delicate drooping branches and lace-like cut foliage.

***B.p.* 'Fastigiata'** A poplar-like tree with columnar shape. Slower-growing than the species.

***B.p.* 'Purpurea'** Also known as PURPLE-LEAVED BIRCH. Taller than the species (23 m/75 ft) with deep purple leaves.

***B.p.* 'Tristis'** Tall graceful narrow tree with weeping branches.

***B.p.* 'Youngii'** Also known as YOUNG'S WEEPING BIRCH. Small tree with pronounced weeping branches. Ideal for small gardens or borders.

B. pubescens DOWNY BIRCH
Z: 4 H: 18 m (60 ft) M
Downy leaves and shoots; papery white bark.

RIGHT *The elegant slender silvery trunks of the Common Silver Birch (* Betula pendula*) look best in small groups or clumps. Here they harmonize well with the architecture of the house nearby. Because their leaf canopy is light and delicate and casts only light shade, silver birches do not seem overbearing even when planted quite close to buildings.*

FAR RIGHT *Young's Weeping Birch (* Betula pendula *'Youngii'), with its small stature and attractive weeping habit, is particularly useful for small gardens. Here it has been used to add height to the planting in a herbaceous and shrub border and effectively punctuates the curve of the bed, screening the garden beyond to create an intriguing air of mystery.*

Cornus

THE CULTIVATED dogwoods are excellent garden trees. Mostly deciduous trees, their wealth of spring blossom rivals that of any other flowering tree and lasts much longer – anything up to four weeks. The massed effect of some of the species of *Cornus* is not created by the flowers but by the bracts that surround them. The *Cornus* genus divides into two groups – those that have numerous small flowers in flat clusters and those whose chief attraction is the shape and colour of the bracts, either four or six to a flower, that surround the small true flowers.

The shape of some of the *Cornus* trees is interesting: a balanced spread of perky upturned branches tipped with buds in winter. Some species offer brilliantly coloured winter stems and many also have the advantage of good autumn foliage colour and occasionally attractive fruits. There are also variegated forms of several *Cornus* species with very attractive yellow- or white-bordered leaves. Most of the species of *Cornus* grow to around 3-6 m (10-20 ft), making them an ideal choice for small gardens, but they look good in larger

RIGHT *The Japanese Dogwood (*Cornus kousa*) makes a rather bushy tree, covered in early summer with four-pointed starry white bracts, set off to perfection by the rich green leaves. Like most of the dogwoods, the leaves turn rich red in autumn.*

LEFT *This American dogwood (*Cornus alternifolia *'Argentea') makes dense layers of neat creamy-variegated foliage, guaranteed to highlight a dark corner, or make good contrast against dark evergreen background planting. The foliage has the bonus of good autumn colour.*

Cornus alba
Z: 5 H: 3 m (10 ft) F
A wide-spreading bush with bright red stems in winter and small white flowers in spring followed by pea-sized bluish-white fruit. ***C.a.* 'Elegantissima'** has particularly attractive creamy-white variegated leaves. ***C.a.* 'Spaethii'** Bright yellow variegated leaves. Red bark in winter. Needs very rich soil.

C. alternifolia
Z: 5 H: 7·5 m (25 ft) S
An American dogwood with wide-spreading branches of attractive foliage and brilliant autumn colour. ***C.a.* 'Argentea'** A white-variegated, slower-growing, smaller form whose foliage is so light that it looks almost like blossom. The flowers themselves are insignificant.

C. capitata BENTHAM'S CORNEL
Z: 8–9 H: 12 m (40 ft) S
A tender evergreen tree with striking sulphur-yellow bracts, about 5 cm (2 in) long and 4 cm ($1\frac{1}{2}$ in) wide, and strawberry-like large fruit.

C. controversa
Z: 5 H: 20 m (65 ft) S
An elegant tree with flat horizontal branches and glossy green leaves. The white flowers are profusely borne in flattish clusters in midsummer, followed by blue-black fruits. ***C.c.* 'Variegata'** has striking yellow-white borders to the leaves.

C. florida FLOWERING DOGWOOD
Z: 5 H: 12 m (40 ft) S
A wide-spreading small tree with beautiful large white bracts in late spring. It also has particularly good autumn foliage colour in shades of red and crimson. ***C.f.* 'Cherokee Chief'** has rich ruby-red bracts in early summer. ***C.f.* 'Pendula'** A form with drooping branches. ***C.f.* 'Rubra'** Deep pink bracts. ***C.f.* 'White Cloud'** Free-flowering variety with creamy-white bracts.

gardens when grouped to create a woodland effect.

A few of the dogwoods will grow into large handsome trees – *Cornus controversa* will eventually reach about 20 m (65 ft), making about 7.5 m (25 ft) in 20 years. The Pacific Dogwood (*C. nuttallii*) has been found in its native north-western America as tall as 30 m (100 ft) although it usually makes no more than 20 m (65 ft) when grown in gardens.

Dogwoods are generally easy to grow, preferring a good well-drained acidic soil that retains moisture. They flower best in full sun but need shelter from prevailing winds. The pink-flowering forms tend to be rather more tender than the others.

ABOVE *A small shrubby tree with pretty cream-edged foliage,* C. mas *'Variegata' also provides attractive yellow flowers in winter, which bloom on the bare stems.*

RIGHT *Some species of dogwood are particularly prized for their long-lasting show of blossom in spring. These pink- and white-flowered varieties,* Cornus florida *'Rubra' and C.f. 'Alba', have been planted close together for maximum value at a time when little else in the garden is in blossom.*

C. kousa JAPANESE DOGWOOD
Z: 5 H: 6 m (20 ft) S
A small bushy tree with slender-pointed, spreading white bracts in early summer and pinkish-red strawberry fruits later. **C.k. 'Chinensis'** A free-flowering form whose blossom covers the branches in summer for weeks on end. Excellent autumn colour. It needs a sunny site and rich well-drained soil.

C. mas CORNELIAN CHERRY
Z: 5 H: 7·5 m (25 ft) S
A small tree with a spreading habit that blooms in late winter producing a wonderful show of yellow flowers on bare branches. Looks best against a backdrop of evergreen foliage. Bright red fruits. **C.m. 'Aurea Elegantissima'** Yellow-, white- or sometimes pink-tinged leaves.

C. nuttallii PACIFIC DOGWOOD
Z: 7 H: 20 m (65 ft) M
One of the best dogwoods for autumn colour, it also carries profuse white bracts in late spring.

C. racemosa
Z: 5 H: 3 m (10 ft) M
A bushy small tree with profuse white flowers in midsummer, followed by small whitish fruit.

C. oblonga
Z: 5 H: 6 m (20 ft) M
Small evergreen tree with scented white flowers in spring. Glossy green leaves.

CRATAEGUS

HAWTHORNS are among the best garden trees, offering the four-fold attractions of interesting heads of dense branches, attractive blossom, fruits and splendid autumn colours, but they have been sadly undervalued by gardeners in the past. There are innumerable species and varieties, some much more worthwhile than others. Their formidably sharp thorns can be used to create a protective vandal- and cat-proof screen to the garden.

Hawthorns have a venerable history. Legend has it that Joseph of Arimathea, visiting England after the crucifixion of Christ, planted his staff in the ground at Glastonbury Abbey. It burst into leaf and flower and the Glastonbury Thorn (*Crataegus monogyna* 'Biflora') is reputed to have flowered on Christmas Day thereafter. Certainly *C.m.* 'Biflora' will often flower at that time of year if the conditions are right.

C. crus-galli COCKSPUR THORN
Z: 5 H: 12 m (40 ft) M-F
A more or less flat-topped tree with spreading branches and dark glossy green leaves. The white flowers in small corymbs have red stamens and pink anthers. Deep-red small round fruit. Its prime virtue, though, is its wonderful autumn colour – a brilliant scarlet – with the bonus that the fruits last throughout the winter.

C. × lavallei
Z: 5 H: 4.5-6 m (15-20 ft) M
Oval glossy green leaves, downy on the undersides, and large white flowers. Orange-red pear-shaped fruits that last all winter.

C. monogyna 'Biflora'
GLASTONBURY THORN
Z: 5 H: 10 m (35 ft) M
Rich polished green foliage and scented white flowers in late spring and again in winter.

C. oxyacantha 'Aurea'
Z: 5 H: 4.5-6 m (15-20 ft) M
This is a yellow-fruited variety of the Common Hawthorn, with glossy green leaves and the customary white flowers in late spring. ***C.o.* 'Paul's Scarlet'** is the best of all red double-flowered thorns. ***C.o.* 'Plena'** has double white flowers which turn pink as they age.

C. phaenopyrum
Z: 5 H: 9 m (30 ft) M
An excellent thorn with a dense round head of leafy branches on a slender trunk, large thorns, and lustrous green leaves. White flowers in midsummer, followed by a wealth of small scarlet fruits that last through the winter. Good autumn colour.

C. prunifolia
Z: 5 H: 6 m (20 ft) M
Round spreading head of branches, brilliant dark green leaves that turn deep crimson in autumn, large white flowers and rich red fruit that falls in autumn.

FAR LEFT *'Paul's Scarlet' is a particularly striking double-flowered form of the hawthorn* Crataegus oxyacantha. *The sight of its profuse clusters of deep pink double flowers against the glossy green foliage in early summer more than makes up for its lack of attractive fruit.*

ABOVE *Like most of the hawthorns,* Crataegus × prunifolia *makes a vivid splash of colour in the garden in autumn.*

LEFT *This small tree earns its place in any garden with its neat habit, glossy green foliage, abundant flowers in spring and its scarlet berries and good foliage colour in autumn. Known as the Washington Hawthorn (*Crataegus phaenopyrum*), it has been planted here with an eye to its maximum impact.*

FRAXINUS

ALONG WITH the oak, most species of Ash (*Fraxinus*) are among the last trees to clothe their winter branches with leaves. But the shivering fern-like foliage, when it finally unfolds, in late spring or even early summer, is a lovely fresh green or, in the case of the rather large white ash, *F. americana*, silver. Their well-spaced branches produce excellent light shade below and attractive patterns against the sky above and, being a hardy and fast-growing species, they are quick to establish themselves. The Ash is not particularly fussy about soil providing it is deep enough to take long roots and despite the subsequent risk to drainage and architectural features and their rather lofty proportions – many mature to between 30 and 45 m (100 and 150 ft) – they are a popular street tree. There are certain types, like the Green Ash, *F. pennsylvanica lanceolata*, and the Velvet Ash, *F. velutina glabra*, which will only achieve 9-12 m (30-40 ft). These, with their excellent wind- and pollution-resistance, make good subjects for urban gardens, and have the bonus of attractive autumn colour.

The wide-spreading roots are a threat not just to underground services but also to nearby shrubs so you may need extra room to keep them apart if you want to grow both. The more decorative forms tend to be smaller and can offer a wide range of foliage colours.

ABOVE RIGHT *With its unusual bell-shaped dome, the fast-growing Weeping Ash (* Fraxinus excelsior 'Pendula'*) makes a good specimen tree. It is, in fact, a graft of the Common Ash (* F. excelsior*).*

RIGHT *As graceful as a ballet dancer, the Manna Ash (* Fraxinus ornus*) has a well-balanced spreading shape and lace-like feathery foliage. The spring flowers are white, while the autumn leaves turn a spectacular pale yellow.*

FAR RIGHT *A pair of more mature Manna Ash trees in autumn, just as the leaves are turning, making a striking contrast with the smooth dark twisted trunk and branches. The attractively dappled shade cast by the Ash makes it an excellent subject for shading a seat, perhaps in the centre of a large lawn.*

Fraxinus angustifolia
NARROW-LEAVED ASH
Z: 7 H: 24.5 m (80 ft) F
An elegant tree with slender pinnate leaves. The smooth dark green foliage provides good dappled shade.

F. excelsior COMMON ASH
Z: 4 H: 30 m (100 ft) F
A fast grower with dark green leaves and a light open canopy of foliage. In autumn the attractive brown winged seeds may produce an irritating proliferation of seedlings later. Prefers an alkaline soil. ***F.e.* 'Diversifolia'** Upright growth; pollution-tolerant. ***F.e.* 'Jaspidea'** Smaller variety with bright yellow shoots, golden autumn colour and bare yellow branches in winter. ***F.e.* 'Pendula'** Wide-spreading branches reach almost to the ground producing an elegant tree.

F. ornus MANNA ASH
Z: 6 H: 15 m (50 ft) M
Like most flowering trees, this is a sun lover, producing fragrant white blossom in spring and dark green foliage. Produces plenty of brown winged seeds that stay on the tree well.

***F. oxycarpa* 'Raywood'**
Z: 6 H: 15 m (50 ft) M
A good light-foliaged tree whose leaves, in drier areas, turn an attractive purple colour in the autumn.

F. pennsylvanica RED ASH
Z: 4 H: 15 m (50 ft) M–F
Lightly furrowed grey bark and graceful long leaves. ***F.p. lanceolata*** Also known as the GREEN ASH, this form has shinier leaves.

F. tomentosa
Z: 6 H: 15 m (50 ft) M
One of the smaller ashes with large furry leaves. Very uncommon in the UK.

F. velutina
Z: 7 H: 12 m (40 ft) M
A slender-trunked ornamental small tree with smaller leaves than most. ***F.v. glabra*** Attractive grey-green velvety leaves.

Hamamelis

PROBABLY BEST known for its magical powers – witch hazel twigs are still preferred for water divining – and for the astringent properties of delicately scented witch hazel lotion, *Hamamelis* is in fact an excellent small tree for gardens of limited size. Most types will make a small bushy tree or shrub with a mass of attractive flowers on the bare winter branches, putting on a pretty display when other trees are often out of season. Except for *H. japonica* 'Arborea', most varieties grow more like shrubs, but *H. mollis* is worth considering also for its autumn colour and sweet-scented flowers in winter. More of a hedgerow or wild species, this is an ideal subject for a small informal or country-style garden, maybe against a background of rowan (*Sorbus*) or hawthorn (*Crataegus*). *Hamamelis* usually prefers a neutral to acid soil and plenty of moisture, although it will thrive both in full sun and shade. Its small size and good pollution-resistance make this a particularly fine choice for town gardens and the flowering shoots can be cut for the house.

BELOW *The Chinese Witch Hazel (*Hamamelis mollis*) is an excellent choice for the foreground of a group of trees, but could equally well be planted as a specimen tree in a corner of a small garden. The scented yellow flowers, borne on bare branches, are an uplifting sight at the end of the winter and the herald of the spring to come.*

LEFT *Hamamelis × intermedia 'Jelena' puts on an eye-catching winter display of bright orange tassels on green speckled branches and stems.*

BELOW *The golden-brown autumn foliage of the Virginian Witch Hazel (Hamamelis virginiana). To get a continuous display, group it with one of the winter-flowering forms, like H. × intermedia 'Jelena' or H. mollis 'Goldcrest'.*

***Hamamelis* × *intermedia* 'Jelena'**
Z: 4 H: 7·5 m (25 ft) S
A variety of *H.* × *intermedia,* itself a hybrid between *H. japonica* and *H. mollis,* ***H.* × *i.* 'Jelena'** has bright copper-orange flowers in dense clusters and good autumn colour.

***H. japonica* 'Arborea'**
JAPANESE WITCH HAZEL
Z: 5 H: 7·5 m (25 ft) S
Pleasant, wide-spreading tree with yellow flowers.

H. mollis CHINESE WITCH HAZEL
Z: 5 H: 7·5 m (25 ft) S
Bushy tree with very fragrant, rich golden-yellow flowers throughout the winter and good yellow autumn foliage colour. Sometimes in bloom on Christmas Day. ***H.m.* 'Goldcrest'** has larger deep golden-yellow flowers, crimson at the base in early spring. ***H.m.* 'Pallida'** Soft sulphur-yellow flowers, profusely borne in late winter.

***H. vernalis* 'Sandra'**
OAK WITCH HAZEL
Z: 4 H: 4·5–7.5 m (15–25 ft) S
Has purplish young leaves, orange, scarlet and flame-red autumn colour and scented yellow flowers from February to March

H. virginiana VIRGINIAN WITCH HAZEL
Z: 4 H: 9 m (30 ft) S
A useful small shrubby tree with downy, oval leaves and small golden-yellow flowers at the same time as the yellow to brown autumn foliage.

ILEX

THE HOLLY must be one of the cheeriest sights through autumn and winter with its glossy, often spiny leaves and (on female plants) bright berries. The bright red against the dark green is a deep-rooted reminder of Christmas and maybe earlier pagan festivals, but there are also excellent variegated golden- and silver-leaved forms, a holly with yellow berries and both evergreen and deciduous types. Their wide range makes them suitable for various roles and positions within both the large and small garden, from the formal clipped *I. aquifolium* to the neat natural pyramid of Perny's Holly, *I. pernyi*, which has small dark green leaves.

LEFT *A very popular hybrid holly,* Ilex × altaclarensis *'Golden King' has bright yellow-variegated leaves, without the customary prickles. Not quite as hardy as some hollies, it nevertheless makes a useful evergreen in sun or semi-shade.*

RIGHT *The elegant appeal of* Ilex × koehneana *'Chestnut Leaf' stems from its unusually slender, pointed, glossy leaves with serrated margins, and its neat, tight clusters of shiny red berries.*

LEFT *A dense-headed evergreen,* Ilex aquifolium *can be clipped into a variety of interesting shapes. The cultivars with variegated leaves,* I.a. *'Argentea' and* I.a. *'Aureomarginata', can be used to produce particularly attractive results.*

RIGHT *Left to its devices,* Ilex aquifolium *'Green Pillar' will grow into a sculptural column of short branches. It has fragrant white flowers in summer, followed by red berries that stay on the tree throughout the winter.*

***Ilex* × *altaclarensis* 'Camelliifolia'**
Z: 7 H: 13·5–21·5 m (45–70 ft) M
Vigorous evergreen hybrid with purple/green foliage and purplish bark. Good-sized berries. ***I.* × *a.* 'Golden King'** Yellow-edged leaves. ***I.* × *a.* 'J. C. van Tol'** Dark green spineless leaves and a mass of red berries. ***I.* × *a.* 'Lawsoniana'** has dark-green-margined, spineless leaves with a central splash of yellow on the female form.

I. aquifolium ENGLISH HOLLY
Z: 7 H: 13·5–21·5 m (45–70 ft) S
Dense glossy green evergreen with small white fragrant flowers and red berries that will stay on the tree right through the year if the birds do not eat them all. Good pollution and salt tolerance. Traditionally popular for clipping into topiary shapes. The variegated varieties are slower growing. ***I.a.* 'Silver Queen'** Creamy-white leaf margins and purple young shoots. It is a male and therefore non-fruiting. ***I.a.* 'Pyramidalis'** is a very freely fruiting variety.

***I. cornuta* 'Burfordii'**
Z: 7 H: 1·5–3 m (4–10 ft) S
Has almost entire leaves and is very free-fruiting.

I.* × *koehneana
Z: 6 H: 15 m (50 ft) S
Particularly long leaves, strongly spined. ***I.* × *k.* 'Chestnut Leaf'** Wavy-edged leaves.

I. pernyi PERNY'S HOLLY
Z: 4 H: 6 m (20 ft) S
A small evergreen tree with dark glossy green leathery leaves and small red berries. Forms an elegant slender pyramid shape when young.

I. verticillata
Z: 4 H: 2–3 m (6–10 ft) S
A bushy deciduous holly with good yellow autumn colour and red berries. Prefers acidic soil.

MAGNOLIA

MAGNOLIAS can be relied upon to herald the coming of better weather with their almost tropical voluptuous waxy flowers, glowing like precious jewels on bare branches. Although young trees are not quick to flower, their shape and foliage is attractive enough to warrant their being positioned as specimen trees right from the outset.

Magnolias fall into three main groups: evergreens, some of which are too large for most gardens; deciduous forms which bloom in summer and whose flowers are partly hidden by the

ABOVE *Delicate as a Chinese watercolour,* Magnolia dawsoniana*'s butterfly-like flowers sit sedately on its narrow bare stems in spring.*

ABOVE RIGHT *The large fragrant white waxy blooms of* Magnolia grandiflora *have a classic appeal, set off to perfection by the glossy dark green foliage. To display itself to best effect,* M. grandiflora *needs plenty of space.*

LEFT Magnolia wilsonii *is one of the smaller magnolias, with the bonus of scented flowers, cup-shaped with dark centres.*

Magnolia cordata
YELLOW CUCUMBER TREE
Z: 5 H: 10 m (35 ft) S
A deciduous magnolia with bright yellow flowers in late summer and early autumn. Its compact upright habit makes it a useful tree where space is restricted.

M. dawsoniana
Z: 5 H: 12 m (40 ft) M
A spreading tree with oval leaves, lustrous green above and downy beneath, emerging after the purple-tinged white flowers, which hang from naked branches in spring. The orange-scarlet fruits are about 10 cm (4 in) long. Frost can damage the flowers and the tree is slow to flower but worth waiting for.

M. grandiflora LAUREL MAGNOLIA
Z: 5 H: 18 m (60 ft) M
The best known of the evergreen species, it has glossy green leaves and scented cream flowers from summer through to autumn. ***M.g.* 'Exmouth'** is a pyramid-shaped tree with large scented creamy blooms and narrow leaves. ***M.g.* 'Gloriosa'** is a particularly spectacular variety with broader leaves and larger flowers. ***M.g.* 'Goliath'** has broad dark green leaves and massive flowers up to 30 cm (12 in) across.

M. liliiflora
Z: 5 H: 4·5 m (15 ft) M
Produces white flowers, purple on the outside, in early summer when the dark green leaves, downy on their undersides, are out. ***M.l.* 'Gracilis'** Slender branches and fastigiate shape. ***M.l.* 'Nigra'** Flowers very dark purple on the outside. It has a neater habit than the species.

RIGHT *For small gardens,* Magnolia × soulangiana *is unbeatable value. Its profuse white flowers on slender branches are a breathtaking sight in early spring.* M. × soulangiana *will flourish even in poor soil, provided it gets plenty of sunshine.*

leaves; and lastly, and most popular of all, the magnolias that bloom in early spring when the leaves are barely open.

The larger evergreen magnolias are best employed as a screen or backdrop against a south- or west-facing wall and the early-blooming magnolias are ideal for small gardens where their singular beauty can be appreciated at close quarters. However, the large buds start to open at the first hint of sunshine so they are at risk from frost damage early in the season.

The flowers of magnolia are easily damaged by winds and heavy rain, so a sheltered spot is best for that reason, too, ideally in front of a wall or in light shade. Magnolias are very tolerant of pollution, making them a good choice for town gardens, but only a few will tolerate limy soil.

M. × ***loebneri*** **'Leonard Messel'**
Z: 5 H: 7·5 m (25 ft) M
Masses of attractive flowers, purplish-pink on the outside and white within, on bare branches in early spring.

M. salicifolia
Z: 5 H: 12 m (40 ft) M
Slender tree with large pure white flowers on naked branches in mid-spring. ***M.s.*** **'Kewensis'** Very fragrant flowers.

M. sinensis CHINESE MAGNOLIA
Z: 6 H: 6 m (20 ft) S
A deciduous summer-flowering tree with large white blooms and sweet-scented oval leaves.

M. × ***soulangiana*** SAUCER MAGNOLIA
Z: 5 H: 7·5 m (25 ft) S
A very popular hybrid with low, spreading branches and white flowers in early spring before the leaves, even on quite young trees. The leaves have good autumn colour. This magnolia will tolerate poor soil and pollution, but will not thrive in chalk or limy soil. There are many varieties; the following is just a short selection: ***M.*** × ***s.*** **'Alba Superba'** has scented white flowers in spring and a useful erect habit. ***M.*** × ***s.*** **'Brozzonii'** has more delicate branches and it flowers a little later than some other magnolias, but its white flowers have attractive purple markings. ***M.*** × ***s.*** **'Lennei'** is a cultivar with attractive large purple flowers with creamy-white centres. ***M.*** × ***s.*** **'Rustica Rubra'** Grows vigorously and has deep red flowers.

M. stellata STAR MAGNOLIA
Z: 5 H: 3 m (10 ft) M
More of a low-growing shrub than a tree, it is nevertheless very attractive with masses of scented double white flowers in spring and it has the advantage that it is small enough to take pride of place in a front garden.

M. wilsonii
Z: 6 H: 7.5 m (25 ft) M
The white cup-shaped flowers are fragrant, hanging from the branches in early summer when they develop alongside the young oval dull green leaves. The flowers are followed by purplish-pink fruit. Does best in part shade.

LEFT Magnolia × loebneri *'Leonard Messel' is one of the most popular magnolias, carrying its flowers on bare branches in early spring. Planting magnolias near a house, especially when the latter provides shelter from cold winds, helps to ensure that early-blooming forms survive with their blossom unscathed.*

LEFT *Seen close up,* Magnolia × loebneri *'Leonard Messel' is one of the loveliest magnolias, with its tight pink buds and pink-streaked white flowers in early spring.*

LEFT *At striking variance to most other magnolias,* M. liliiflora *'Nigra' has large, deep-purple-shaded velvety flowers set off by the attractive shiny green leaves.*

FAR LEFT *The Star Magnolia (*Magnolia stellata*) is usually more of a shrub than a tree, but its tiny domed shape and mass of white star-shaped flowers in early spring makes it an ideal specimen for small or front gardens or as the centrepiece in a small lawn.*

MALUS

FEW TREES are as ideally suited to the small garden as the crab apple, blessed as it is with the most beautiful scented blossom in spring, a mass of bright fruits in autumn, a pretty spreading shape and, sometimes, good autumn colour. The leaves tend to be small, simple and toothed in various shades of green, from gold- to purple-tinged.

The blossom is early and eye-catching, a mass of creamy-white, pale or dark pink, that completely smothers the branches. The fruits make an invaluable blaze of autumn colour; they may be as large as plums or as small as berries and come in many different shades: yellow, scarlet, purple or blushed with pink.

It is easy to grow, hardier than cherries and will tolerate most soils and cold winter weather. It likes the sun and matures at a modest height of between 3 and 7.5 m (10 and 25 ft), although some may grow taller. Young trees should be pruned in winter or early spring.

ABOVE *It is easy to see how this Cherry Crab Apple (*Malus × *'Robusta') has earned its name. Although the fruits appear only every other year, their colour and abundance are worth the wait. As a bonus, the spring flowers are sweetly scented.*

LEFT *Fleeting in its appeal admittedly, an apple orchard in full bloom in spring is one of the delights of the countryside. The crops of apples in late summer and early autumn make up for the briefness of its flowering season.*

RIGHT *This Japanese flowering crab apple has been specially developed for its spring blossom. The fruits of* Malus floribunda *are small but the flowers are prolific, completely masking the branches with reddish buds and scented pink blooms in spring.*

M. baccata SIBERIAN CRAB
Z: 3 H: 15 m (50 ft) M
A very hardy round-headed tree with an upright habit when young. The spring flowers are white and sweetly scented; very small red or yellow fruits in autumn. ***M.b.* 'Columnaris'** Useful, compact columnar shape.

M. domestica *(M. pumila)*
Z: 3 H: 7·5 m (25 ft) M
There are numerous cultivars and varieties of the orchard apple. 'Family' trees often have three varieties on one rootstock – an excellent choice for small gardens.

M. floribunda
Z: 5 H: 7·5 m (25 ft) M
Masses of rosy-red buds and pale pink flowers in spring; yellow fruits.

M. hupehensis
Z: 4 H: 7·5 m (25 ft) M
Pink/white spring flowers, yellow-red fruits in autumn.

***M.* 'John Downie'**
Z: 4 H: 7·5 m (25 ft) M
Pink-budded flowers, opening white. Profuse clusters of orange conical fruit.

***M.* 'Red Jade'**
Z: 4 H: 6 m (20 ft) M
White flowers in spring, red fruit alternate years. Pendulous habit.

***M.* × 'Robusta'** CHERRY CRAB APPLE
Z: 4 H: 7·5 m (25 ft) M
White spring flowers and long-lasting showy red fruits in autumn.

M. tschonoskii
Z: 6 H: 12 m (40 ft) M-F
A Japanese Crab with excellent autumn colour – the foliage turns red, yellow and orange. The flowers are pinky-white and the fruits yellow with a purple or red tinge. They soon drop.

PINUS

THE SHARP evergreen needles and large uncompromising conical shape of the pine have given it a rather poor reputation recently through its unsympathetic use within smaller garden schemes. Too many pines, too close to the house, are indeed threatening and depressing, depriving us of any sense of the changing seasons and uncomfortably reminiscent of giant disapproving sentinels. However, judiciously positioned among other, lighter trees, they add useful tall flat-topped or pyramidal shapes and an excellent choice of densely packed foliage colour from deep greens and golds to greys and blues. Often the new foliage in summer produces charming light tips to brighten the regularity.

Their major assets are their fresh, almost fruity aroma and the beautiful range of cones. Some species are ideally suited to a coastal climate making them a distinctive feature of the scenery: you can achieve a Mediterranean effect by choosing one of the hardier, grey-green types as a background for more tender shrubs and herbs in a sheltered garden.

Pines are also a popular subject for bonsai (see page 86) where a small shallow trough can be converted into a delightful pine grove.

RIGHT *Pines need not look gloomy by the pool-side as this* Pinus nigra (P. austriaca) *handsomely demonstrates with its light green fingers of new growth pointing skywards. The feathery branches trailing into the water make a good visual link between the bank and the pool.*

LEFT *Aromatic foliage and a wonderful variety of shape, size and colour are the pine family's main claims to garden worthiness. The smaller forms look best planted in closely related, contrasting groups to produce a patchwork of colour. Here the spiny foliage is graduated downwards from the blue-green Bosnian Pine (*Pinus leucodermis*) to the bright green Scots Pine (*P. sylvestris*), matched at ground level by the Golden Heather (*Calluna vulgaris *'Golden Haze').*

RIGHT *Proving that pines are more than just useful evergreens, this young growth of* Pinus parviflora *'Brevifolia' makes a striking display of bright green against the blue of the mature branches and the amazing raspberry-like strobili.*

FAR RIGHT *The Bristlecone Pine (*Pinus aristata*), with its curious arrangement of stiff bristly branches and light brown cones, is worth growing as a specimen.*

Pinus aristata BRISTLECONE PINE
Z: 6 H: 15 m (50 ft) S
A distinctive bushy pine ideal for small gardens. Closely packed leaves and bristly cones (hence the tree's common name).

P. densiflora JAPANESE RED PINE
Z: 4 H: 21·5-36 m (70-120 ft) M
Interesting crooked shape and purple/pink cones. Tolerant of sea spray.

***P. heldreichii* 'Leucodermis'**
Z: 6 H: 15 m (50 ft) S-M
Handsome dense-leaved pine with a narrow habit. Dark green foliage and blue-brown cones. Withstands winds; lime-tolerant.

P. nigra maritima CORSICAN PINE
Z: 4 H: 12-42 m (40-140 ft) M
Another grey-green pine which will tolerate most soils, including chalk, as well as coastal conditions.

P. parviflora
Z: 5 H: 15 m (50 ft) S
Bushy pine with dark needles and masses of cones.

P. pinaster MARITIME PINE
Z: 7 H: 27·5-36 m (90-120 ft) M
A useful coastal tree for a warm climate which tolerates sandy soil. The pretty female flowers on the shoot tips are red.

P. pinea STONE PINE
Z: 8 H: 24·5 m (80 ft) M
Interesting for its unusual flat-topped foliage on top of a tall stem, looking very like a parasol or umbrella. Suitable only for mild areas.

P. sylvestris SCOTS PINE
Z: 2 H: 27·5 m (90 ft) M
A huge stately tree which has blue-green foliage with brighter tips and, when mature, attractive orange-brown peeling bark, especially in the crown. ***P.s.* 'Aurea'** is a slow-growing cultivar with good yellow foliage colour throughout the winter.

PRUNUS

THIS GENUS comprises not only the ever-popular flowering cherries, but some of the best edible fruit trees too – cherry, plum, peach and almond. From an ornamental point of view the flowering cherries are second only to crab apples in garden worthiness. They are mostly compact in size and offer the bonus of delicate, papery flowers in every shade from white to cerise, some scented, some single, some double.

Some flowering cherries have attractive foliage as well so it is worth choosing one of these. The majority are fast-growing and bloom when still young. They will grow reasonably easily on most well-drained soils. Shapes can vary from round, spreading and flat-topped to weeping. The Japanese have selected some varieties to produce a purple or bronze tinge to the foliage and a few, like the Sargent Cherry, *P. sargentii*, have good autumn colour as a bonus. There is a particularly good cherry which blooms in autumn and winter – *P. subhirtella* 'Autumnalis'.

Peach, almond and apricot are all worth growing for their crops if you have a warm enough situation for them. Although the almond will not fruit in colder climates, it produces a wonderful early display of delicate white blossom.

BELOW *A vast spread of large double flowers in drooping clusters is the main attraction of* Prunus *'Shimidsu'. Like most of the Japanese garden cherries, its blossom-laden branches make a striking contrast with the plain dark stems and light green foliage.*

RIGHT *Two forms of Japanese cherry, both pink-flowered, make an exciting contrast of form. On the left,* Prunus *'Kiku Shidare Zakura' has a lax, weeping habit, its blossom dangling from the branches.* Prunus *'Kanzan' on the right has deeper pink clusters of flowers on upright branches.*

FLOWERING CHERRIES
***Prunus* 'Accolade'**
Z: 5 H: 9 m (30 ft) M
A cross between *P. sargentii* and *P. subhirtella*, this is a useful small tree producing a mass of semi-double pink blooms in early spring.

P. avium WILD CHERRY
Z: 4 H: 21·5 m (70 ft) F
Small white flowers in spring, good red autumn colour and small black fruit. It makes a tall pyramid shape. ***P.a.* 'Plena'** Small double white flowers in spring.

P. padus BIRD CHERRY
Z: 4 H: 15 m (50 ft) M
Almond-scented drooping racemes of white flowers adorn the tree in late spring. It has a spreading habit and strings of small black fruits in summer. Varieties have different coloured foliage.

P. sargentii SARGENT CHERRY
Z: 5 H: 12 m (40 ft) M
Prized for its clusters of deep pink flowers in early spring and good bronze-red autumn foliage colour. Has a good upright shape.

***P. subhirtella* 'Autumnalis'**
AUTUMN CHERRY
Z: 6 H: 9 m (30 ft) M
Valuable for its show of white semi-double flowers in winter; new blossom appears again in spring. ***P.s.* 'Rosea'** has pink flowers. ***P.s.* 'Pendula'** is a weeping form with tiny pink flowers in early spring.

JAPANESE GARDEN CHERRIES
***P.* 'Amanogawa'**
Z: 4 H: 9 m (30 ft) M
Very upright habit, and fragrant pink semi-double flowers in early spring, followed by small black fruits. The young foliage has a yellow tinge.

***P.* 'Kanzan'**
Z: 4 H: 12 m (40 ft) F
A vigorous spreading tree with crimson buds in mid-spring, opening rose-pink.

P. 'Kiku Shidare Zakura'
Z: 5 H: 7·5 m (25 ft) M
Weeping cherry with very double pink flowers in mid spring.

P. 'Shimidsu' (*P.* 'Shimidsu Zakura')
Z: 5 H: 7·5 m (25 ft) M
Flowers pink in bud, opening pure white in mid-spring, semi-double in long pendulous corymbs.

P. 'Shirofugen'
Z: 6 H: 7·5 m (25 ft) M
A wonderful tree for variety of colour; the young foliage has a bronze tinge, the buds open purple in early summer and then cover the branches in clusters of pink and white flowers.

FRUITING TREES

P. armeniaca APRICOT
Z: 5 H: 6 m (20 ft) S
Can sometimes be grown on a south-facing wall in colder climates, otherwise blossom killed by spring frosts.

P. cerasus SOUR CHERRY
Z: 5 H: 6 m (20 ft) M
Pure white flowers in spring and red to blackish juicy acid fruits in early autumn. ***P.c.* 'Austera'** is the MORELLO CHERRY, with superior dark-coloured fruit.

P. dulcis ALMOND
Z: 7 H: 9 m (30 ft) S–M
Produces a fine display of delicate white blossom in very early spring. Fruit needs sunshine and warmth to ripen. Needs well-drained soil.

P. persica PEACH
Z: 5 H: 7·5 m (25 ft) M
Pink spring blossom and narrow matt green leaves; luscious edible fruits. Best grown on a south-facing wall.

P. spinosa SLOE, BLACKTHORN
Z: 5 H: 3 m (10 ft) M–F
A small shrubby tree with spiny branches and pure white flowers, often on naked wood, in early spring. Blue-black fruits. Best for screening and hedging.

LEFT *The fruiting cherries still produce the same splendid light-against-dark effect of the Japanese cherries, although the blossom is less profusely borne. The impact here comes from the rows of* Prunus *'St. Bris le Vineux', with their bonus of luscious edible fruit in summer.*

BELOW *Laden with early spring flowers, the drooping branches of* Prunus serrulata *'Cheal's Weeping Cherry' reach almost to the ground.*

LEFT *Wild cherries can be both decorative and practical. The Blackthorn (*Prunus spinosa*) is a vigorous spreading shrubby tree with the advantage of edible blue-black berries (they make good jelly or liqueur). Beware, however, of the particularly vicious thorns.*

QUERCUS

THE VENERABLE OAK has its roots well entwined in history and a formidable reputation as a stalwart member of the forests of Europe and North America. Although many of the large oaks are too slow-growing for most gardens, there are many ornamental and fast-growing species like the Red Oak (*Quercus rubra*) that are worth considering for the garden. The Turkey Oak (*Q. cerris*) is another fast grower; others, like the Holm Oak (*Q. ilex*), withstand sea spray. It is a tough evergreen and being tall and slim it makes a good boundary tree. It can also be clipped into hedges or ornamental shapes. There are many others which can offer interesting leaf shapes, good autumn colour or attractive broad spreading heads of branches.

*The Turkey Oak (*Quercus cerris*) is a good subject for an exposed site where it makes a round-headed tree with a shortish trunk. Unlike most other members of its family, it will tolerate chalky soil.*

RIGHT *These American red oaks (*Quercus rubra*) provide a shady rich green screen and shelter for the house, linking the garden to an informal wooded area beyond.*

Quercus alba WHITE OAK
Z: 4 H: 30 m (100 ft) M–F
Deciduous oak with good autumn colour. In time it develops a stately broad spreading form.

Q. cerris TURKEY OAK
Z: 7 H: 33 m (110 ft) M–F
A fast-growing oak and one which will tolerate pollution, chalk and coastal conditions.

Q. × hispanica
Z: 7 H: 30 m (100 ft) M–F
Lime-tolerant with a good round head of branches. ***Q. × h.* 'Crispa'** is an almost evergreen form.

Q. ilex HOLM or HOLLY OAK
Z: 7 H: 24·5 m (80 ft) S–M
A broad evergreen with narrow glossy green leaves. Can be clipped.

BELOW *The Golden Oak (*Quercus robur *'Concordia') makes a handsome small tree, but is rather slow growing.*

Q. palustris PIN OAK
Z: 5 H: 30 m (100 ft) M–F
A dense head of elegant slender branches and good red autumn colours.

Q. robur ENGLISH or COMMON OAK
Z: 5 H: 30 m (100 ft) M–F
Long-lived deciduous oak with a short trunk and wide head of branches. Its cultivars are a better choice for smaller gardens: the PURPLE ENGLISH OAK (**Q.r. 'Atropurpurea'**), the GOLDEN OAK (**Q.r. 'Concordia'**) or the slow-growing variegated **Q.r. 'Variegata'**.

Q. rubra RED OAK
Z: 5 H: 24·5 m (80 ft) M–F
This round-headed tree grows quite fast and has excellent autumn colour. It prefers acidic soil.

Q. suber CORK OAK
Z: 8 H: 18 m (60 ft) M–F
Small oak with attractive rough bark and glossy evergreen leaves. Likes a sunny position and shelter from wind.

RHODODENDRON

HANDSOME EVERGREENS, all rhododendrons are lime-haters, growing best in an acid soil and in light shade. They are a moisture-loving species and although the smaller forms make attractive underplanting for trees, they will lose out in the battle for water if planted too close to greedy trees like elms, beeches, limes, birches and sycamores. They will succeed in the shade of most ornamental garden trees. Since the most attractive feature of the rhododendron is its flowers, grow them where they can be appreciated. There are hundreds to choose from, some delightfully fragrant.

R. arboreum
Z: 7 H: 12 m (40 ft) M
One of the tallest rhododendrons in the wild with dense heads of about twenty flowers in shades of white or pink. Long dark leathery evergreen leaves.
R.a. campbelliae Blood-red flowers.

R. augustinii
Z: 5 H: 6 m (20 ft) M
Flowers in late spring/early summer with rose-purple trusses with olive blotches. May not flower well in cool gardens. ***R.a.* 'Rubra'** Red flowers.
***R.a.* 'Electra'** Violet-blue flowers.

R. hodgsonii
Z: 7 H: 7·5 m (25 ft) M
An evergreen shrub or small tree, it has particularly handsome leaves and attractive peeling bark. The rose-lilac or magenta-purple flowers are packed tightly into rounded trusses.

R. pentaphyllum
Z: 7 H: 6 m (20 ft) M
A deciduous tree-like azalea with small leaves and large solitary rose-pink flowers in late spring. The leaves turn rich orange and crimson in autumn.

R. ponticum
Z: 6 H: 7·5 m (25 ft) F
Dark green evergreen leaves and heads of light purple flowers in late spring. Makes a useful windbreak or informal hedge but it can be invasive.

HYBRIDS
***R.* 'King George'** A clone of *R.* 'Loderi' with flowers blush-tinted at first, becoming white.
***R.* 'Loderi'** Nine to twelve large fragrant flowers in tall trusses, white to blush- or light pink. Medium green leaves. A vigorous grower that flowers freely in shelter and light shade.
***R.* 'Loder's White'** Pure white flowers in late spring. Hardy and vigorous.
***R.* 'Naomi'** Delicate fragrant pink flowers in late spring.

LEFT *Rhododendrons look best in an informal woodland setting with a backdrop of light-foliaged trees behind. Subtle colour harmonies always look better than strong contrasts, as* Rhododendron augustinii *(shown in close-up far left, below) and* R. *'King George' (far left, above) shown here prove.*

ROBINIA

ROBINIAS are deciduous, ornamental trees, fast-growing if given plenty of sun. They will do well even in poor soil (but not on chalk) and in polluted towns, but the brittle branches are likely to be damaged by strong winds. However it is not just their tolerance that makes them such popular garden trees. The fern-like leaves make a welcome fresh green canopy, casting dappled shade in which grass will grow easily, so they are ideal for shading a corner of the garden, or for positioning close to a patio or path. In summer there are drooping racemes of pink, white or purple flowers, sometimes fragrant, and in autumn the leaves turn pale yellow. Generally, the *Robinia* is an undemanding, pretty tree for a dull corner or a lawn, but there are several species that can be relied upon to add more of a dramatic note to your garden scheme: *R. pseudacacia* 'Frisia' produces brilliant golden-yellow foliage from spring to autumn and a dense compact canopy of bright feathery leaves that is guaranteed to add life and colour among more sombre trees and shrubs. The rough, deeply furrowed bark and random branches of the species tree, *R. pseudacacia*, are also useful for winter interest.

Robinia hartwigii
Z: 4 H: 3·6 m (12 ft) M
Abundant white to rose-purple flowers in midsummer, feathery foliage and long downy seed-pods.

R. hispida ROSE ACACIA
Z: 7 H: 2·5 m (8 ft) S–M
An arboreal thornless shrub with typical divided leaves and showy deep rose-coloured racemes of flowers. Needs some shelter.

R. kelseyi
Z: 5 H: 4·5 m (15 ft) M
Profuse rose-coloured flowers in summer and handsome red seed-pods.

R. pseudacacia LOCUST, FALSE ACACIA
Z: 4 H: 21·5 m (70 ft) F
Fragrant white flowers in early summer, thorns either side of each leaf bud and rough bark providing winter interest. Good pollution resistance. ***R.p.* 'Aurea'** Yellow leaves that turn green later. ***R.p.* 'Frisia'** A very vigorous tree with bright golden-yellow foliage most of the growing season. ***R.p.* 'Pyramidalis'** Good columnar form for restricted space and dry soil but its flowers are sparse. ***R.p.* 'Umbraculifera'** Also known as MOP-HEAD or PARASOL ACACIA. Small slower-growing tree with compact round head.

FAR LEFT *Robinias make excellent garden trees, their feathery foliage creating only the lightest shade.* Robinia pseudacacia *'Frisia' is widely grown for its striking golden-yellow foliage which creates a welcome splash of colour throughout the growing season.*

LEFT *The fresh feathery leaves of the False Acacia or Black Locust (* Robinia pseudacacia *'Umbraculifera') can be grown into slender-stemmed lollipop shapes for creating avenues, light shelter or, as here, to mark the boundaries of a small seating area within an informal garden.*

Sorbus

LEFT *The silvery undersides of the leaves of* Sorbus aria *'Lutescens', planted here in a group, have wonderful light-reflecting qualities. Its slender form makes it a good choice for smaller gardens.*

RIGHT *The Service Tree (*Sorbus domestica*) grows to around 18 m (60 ft), making a wide-spreading dome of fine foliage. This variety, S.m. 'Maliformis' in Kew Gardens, puts on a glorious display of flaming autumn colour, and deserves the prominent position it has been given.*

This large genus offers all things for all gardens and something for every season. The rowans, which comprise a large part of the genus, are handsome trees, often with fresh fern-like foliage producing light shade, compact habit and brilliant displays of autumn colour. Their wealth of conspicuous berries is a prominent feature. Rowans can stand alone as specimen trees but are small enough to be grouped together to create a small-scale woodland. The autumn berries come in a range of colours – pink, orange, deep or pale yellow, even white – and are borne in generous clusters. They last throughout the winter, if the birds do not plunder them first, or if you do not harvest them yourself to make excellent tart jelly or jam.

The Whitebeams (*Sorbus aria*), occasionally called Service Trees, get their name from the felt or furry greyish-white undersides of their leaves, which help to lighten the effect of the foliage, and in sunlight they seem to shimmer silver. As a result they look particularly attractive with darker green leaves as a backdrop, or grouped with golden-leaved trees for a stunning combination of silver and gold. There are many different forms, some with deeply lobed leaves and others with fruit as big as crab apples. The flowers are often delightfully fragrant.

S. americana
AMERICAN MOUNTAIN ASH
Z: 3 H: 4·5–9 m (15–30 ft) M
Narrow pinnate leaves, white flowers and round red fruits that stay on the bare branches all winter. Does best in acid soil.

S. aria WHITEBEAM
Z: 5 H: 9–12 m (30–40 ft) M
Pale green oval leaves with white hairy undersides, scented white flowers and red fruits. Good golden autumn foliage. An excellent tree for chalky soil. ***S.a.* 'Lutescens'** Conical habit; silvery leaves.

S. aucuparia ROWAN, MOUNTAIN ASH
Z: 3 H: 20 m (65 ft) M
Fern-like leaves with red autumn colour, white flowers in spring and clusters of red berries from autumn through to spring. ***S.a.* 'Beissneri'** has coppery-brown branches and trunk, yellowish leaves and yellow fruit in autumn. ***S.a.* 'Sheerwater Seedling'** has a very upright growth and ***S.a.* 'Xanthocarpa'** has yellow fruits.

S. domestica SERVICE TREE
Z: 5 H: 18 m (60 ft) M
Scaly bark, typically feathery foliage and white flowers in late spring. Good bronze autumn tints and pear- or apple-shaped edible fruit.

LEFT *Rowans are known for their end-of-season colour, and* Sorbus *'Embley' pictured here is one of the best. The rich scarlet of the leaves, with the bright berries, is a visual feast in autumn.*

S. 'Embley'
Z: 3 H: 10 m (35 ft) M
Graceful large leaflets that turn a good colour in autumn and bright red fruit.

S. 'Joseph Rock'
Z: 6 H: 12 m (40 ft) M
One of the most popular varieties with upright habit and vibrant autumn colour. Pale yellow berries.

S. meliosmifolia
Z: 6 H: 10 m (35 ft) M
Abundant hawthorn-scented flowers in late spring and bronze-coloured fruit.

A-Z of Useful Garden Trees

Abies
A. delavayi
Z: 7-8 H: 12 m (40 ft) M-F
Dense foliage with silver undersides. Dark blue cones.

A. koreana KOREAN FIR
Z: 5 H: 12-18 m (40-60 ft) S
Good conical shape although sometimes grows short and bushy. White-striped effect leaves give it fresh green appeal. Pointed purple cones.

Acacia
A. dealbata MIMOSA, SILVER WATTLE
Z: 9 H: 15 m (50 ft) F
Attractive fern-like leaves are silver-green and the yellow clusters of flowers fragrant, appearing late winter. Produces blue seed pods. Prefers sun. ***A.d.* 'Decurrens'** Rich green leaves.

Acer (see page 102)

Aesculus (see page 106)

Ailanthus
A. altissima TREE OF HEAVEN
Z: 5 H: 15-21 m (50-70 ft) F
A useful, usually modest-sized tree to about 15 m (50 ft), which is tolerant of dry shade and an acid soil. Male and female yellowish flowers are carried on separate trees – the male flowers smell rather unpleasant. Female trees produce a mass of red-brown winged seeds. If they are cut down, they are liable to produce prolific root suckers.

Albizia
A. julibrissin SILK TREE, PINK SIRIS
Z: 8 H: 12 m (40 ft) F
Broad-spreading tree with pretty round pink flowers in summer and seed pods in autumn. Will produce several trunks unless pruned when young into a single stem. Attractive feathery leaves create light shade that is perfect for patios or lawns. Will produce flowers while still young. Tolerates strong wind, some shade and alkaline soil, but prefers a position in full sun.

Alnus
A. cordata ITALIAN ALDER
Z: 5 H: 24·5 m (80 ft) F
A conical tree with bright glossy green leaves and spring catkins. Grows well in any type of soil but, like all alders, enjoys a damp position, maybe near a pond. Unlike most other alders, will tolerate a lime soil.

A. glutinosa COMMON ALDER
Z: 4 H: 24·5 m (80 ft) F
Narrow pyramidal tree for damp ground with long yellow male flowers and erect small red female ones. Early spring catkins have a purple tinge as do new shoots. Ripe fruits in autumn look like little brown cones. ***A.g.* 'Aurea'** A golden-yellow form making a splash of colour in spring and summer; ***A.g.* 'Laciniata'** Tough dainty smaller form with slender lobed leaves.

A. incana GREY ALDER
Z: 2 H: 20 m (65 ft) F
Useful medium-sized tree for a damp, cold position. Sometimes grows more like a large shrub. Leaves grey-green and downy. ***A.i.* 'Aurea'** Yellow form with red-tinged catkins; ***A.i.* 'Laciniata'** Particularly hardy form with grey dissected foliage.

A. rubra (*A. oregona*) RED ALDER
Z: 3 H: 12-15 m (40-50 ft) M
More commonly grown in the USA than the UK. Has dark green leaves with rust-red/grey undersides and a light grey-white bark. Makes a narrow conical shape.

Amelanchier
A. laevis (*A. canadensis*)
Z: 5 H: 12 m (40 ft) S
Blooms early in spring with massed clusters of white flowers. A shrubby tree with delicate branches, simple dark green leaves tinged with purple when young and in early summer tiny black berries sweet enough to eat and very attractive to birds. A hardy tree that prefers moist lime-free soil but will

Arbutus × andrachnoides

thrive almost anywhere in full sun or light shade.

A. lamarckii (*A.* × *grandiflora*)
Z: 5 H: 6-9 m (20-30 ft) S
A popular species with masses of white flowers, good autumn colour and small purplish berries. Grows well on a very chalky soil.

ARALIA

A. elata JAPANESE ANGELICA TREE
Z: 3 H: 9-15 m (30-50 ft) S
Good value for small gardens. Huge clusters of white flowers in late summer and autumn and large green leaves made up of many leaflets rather like angelica leaves borne on mainly unbranched spiny shoots. Will often grow into a suckering shrub. Hardy, though may be damaged by spring frosts and grows in sun or light shade. The two variegated forms are extremely decorative but difficult to get hold of. ***A.e.* 'Aureo-variegata'** A yellow-cream variegated version. Shows its colour best in a sunny position; ***A.e.* 'Variegata'** Foliage has green and white variegation.

ARAUCARIA

A. araucana CHILE PINE, MONKEY PUZZLE TREE
Z: 7 H: 15-24·5 m (50-80 ft) S-M
An unusual-looking evergreen with a tall, very straight, scarred trunk of dark grey, topped with a wide-spreading head of tangled branches. Produces large interesting cones and tolerates all but extreme soil conditions. Needs a lot more room than most trees and is usually best planted as an isolated specimen.

ARBUTUS

A.* × *andrachnoides
Z: 8 H: 6-9 m (20-30 ft) S
Attractive hybrid of the Strawberry Tree with striking reddish branches, dark green leaves and clusters of white flowers in spring or autumn. Lime-tolerant.

Aralia elata **'Aureo-variegata'**

A. unedo STRAWBERRY TREE
Z: 8 H: 12 m (40 ft) S
Clusters of flowers in late autumn with lime-green, later pink, rough strawberry-like fruits that ripen in the following autumn as the next flowers appear. Lime-tolerant. ***A.u.* 'Rubra'** Pink-red flowered form with plenty of fruits.

AZARA
A. integrifolia
Z: 9 H: 6 m (20 ft) M
Glossy evergreen leaves and fragrant flowers with purple sepals and rich yellow stamens in late winter to early spring, producing mauve-stained white berries.

BETULA (see page 108)

BUDDLEIA
B. alternifolia BUTTERFLY BUSH
Z: 6 H: 4·5 m (15 ft) M
Delicate arching branches laden with tiny mauve scented flowers in summer. Can be trained against a wall or grown as a standard.

B. davidii
Z: 6 H: 4·5 m (15 ft) F
Purple flower spikes. One of the most popular shrubs with butterflies. Cut right back every spring to encourage new flowering stems. Varieties have blue, red or white flowers.

BUXUS
B. sempervirens COMMON BOX
Z: 6 H: 4·5-9 m (15-30 ft) S
A slow-growing evergreen with tiny dark green shiny leaves, perfect for clipping into shrub or topiary shapes. Will tolerate most soils, especially pure chalk, and sun or shade.

CALLISTEMON
C. citrinus BOTTLE BRUSH
Z: 9 H: 4·5 m (15 ft) M
Small tree, commonly grown as a shrub, with lemon-scented leaves and spectacular bottle brushes of red or yellow flowers followed by interesting spikes of round seeds. A member of the myrtle family, it is most frequently seen in Australia.

Catalpa bignonioides

CAMELLIA
C. japonica
Z: 7 H: 6 m (20 ft) S-M
A small evergreen tree or shrub producing a mass of enormous single or double flowers which range from white through pink to red. Will tolerate shade and prefers the shelter of another tree or wall but not facing morning sun as this damages the buds. Needs a lime-free soil. There is a great range of different varieties.

C. reticulata
Z: 9 H: 10·5 m (35 ft) S
A tender form but with larger and more brilliant red flowers in early spring. Best fan trained.

C. sasanqua
Z: 7 H: 6 m (20 ft) S
Fragrant white flowers in early winter. Needs shelter. Cultivated varieties have large red or pink, and sometimes double, flowers.

C.* × *williamsii
Z: 7 H: 6 m (20 ft) S-M
Generally extremely floriferous and vigorous as the dead flowers fall off rather than staying on the bush.

CARAGANA
C. arborescens SIBERIAN PEA TREE
Z: 2 H: 6 m (20 ft) S
Extremely tough small tree from Siberia with clusters of yellow pea-like flowers in spring and later, small pea pods. A good wind-break tree tolerating all soils and most positions.

CARPINUS
C. betulus COMMON HORNBEAM
Z: 5 H: 15-24·5 m (50-80 ft) M
Dark green deciduous tree with dense foliage very suitable for clipping into hedges or formal shapes. Good yellow autumn colour and smooth grey bark. Prefers full sun. ***C.b.* 'Columnaris'** Smaller slow-growing form with compact upright shape. ***C.b.* 'Fastigiata'** Produces a dense oval shape that looks naturally clipped and spreads more than its name suggests. ***C.b.* 'Incisa'** Small, deeply toothed leaves.

C. cordata
Z: 5 H: 12-15 m (40-50 ft) S
Attractive furry, quilted, heart-shaped leaves and scaly bark. Also has decorative catkins and small green fruits.

CARYA

C. cordiformis BITTERNUT HICKORY
Z: 5 H: 27·5 m (90 ft) M
A hardy tree for winter interest – the buds are covered with yellow scales. Has good yellow autumn colour and clusters of pear-shaped fruits. Does best in good soil.

C. glabra PIGNUT HICKORY
Z: 5 H: 18 m (60 ft) F
Yellow autumn colour, grey bark and edible nuts.

C. ovata SHAGBARK HICKORY
Z: 4 H: 24·5 m (80 ft) F
Upright oval habit, flaking grey bark and golden autumn colour.

C. tomentosa BIGBUD HICKORY, MOCKERNUT HICKORY
Z: 5 H: 27·5 m (90 ft) M
Rarely cultivated tree with round head, long, very downy catkins and round fruits. Large winter buds (hence the common name) and fragrant leaves.

CASTANEA

C. dentata
AMERICAN SWEET CHESTNUT
Z: 5 H: 30 m (100 ft) M
Dull-green tapered leaves, catkins and spiny husked nuts.

C. sativa SPANISH CHESTNUT, SWEET CHESTNUT
Z: 6 H: 30 m (100 ft) F
Yellowish flowers put on a good display and the tapering foliage makes this a good shade tree. Nuts edible and variable in size. Prefers a non-alkaline soil and full sun. Will resist drought. ***C.s.* 'Aureo-marginata'** Leaves have yellow borders. Much smaller tree. ***C.s.* 'Marron de Lyon'** Early but large fruiting variety.

CATALPA

C. bignonioides INDIAN BEAN TREE
Z: 5 H: 15 m (50 ft) F
A deceptively fast-growing, wide-spreading tree popular for its shade and pollution resistance. Foliage is fresh green and the white-spotted-with-purple summer flowers are attractive. Flowers are followed by brown seed pods. Mature specimens develop gnarled branches. ***C.b.* 'Aurea'** Also known as the GOLDEN INDIAN BEAN TREE. No more than 6-9 m (20-30 ft). Prized for its excellent golden foliage.

***C. × erubescens* 'J. C. Teas'**
Z: 5 H: 18 m (60 ft) M
New foliage has a purple tinge. Flowers smaller than *C. bignonioides* but more numerous, white with yellow staining and purple spots. May be difficult to find. ***C. × e.* 'Purpurea'** Early shoots and foliage dark purple, almost black. May also be difficult to find.

C. fargesii
Z: 5 H: 9-18 m (30-60 ft) S
Smaller leaves and fine, pinkish summer flowers with yellow and rust markings, producing long seed pods.

C. ovata
Z: 5 H: 12 m (40 ft) M
Lobed leaves and small white flowers with red and yellow markings.

C. speciosa WESTERN CATALPA
Z: 4 H: 15-18 m (50-60 ft) M
Heart-shaped leaves and large white flowers. Generally makes a more upright tree than *C. bignonioides*.

CEANOTHUS

C. arboreus CALIFORNIAN LILAC, CATALINA CEANOTHUS
Z: 8 H: 4·5-6 m (15-20 ft) M
A bushy evergreen, usually grown against walls. Pretty blue flowers, black seed pods and tiny evergreen foliage. Likes a sunny, sheltered position. ***C.a.* 'Trewithen Blue'** is particularly attractive.

***Camellia sasanqua* 'Papaver'**

Buddleia davidii

Chamaecyparis lawsoniana, C.l. **'Aurea Densa'**, *C.i.* **'Elwoodii'** *and C.l.* **'Obtusa Crispii'**

Cladrastis lutea

C. thyrsiflorus
Z: 7 H: 6 m (20 ft) M
A hardier evergreen with bright blue flowers in summer, it is also a good wall shrub. ***C.t.*** **'Cascade'** is hardier and has even better flower colour.

CEDRUS
C. atlantica ATLAS CEDAR
Z: 6-7 H: 36 m (120 ft) M-F
Forms a hardy evergreen pyramid of glossy leaves varying from green to silvery. Long, cylindrical and erect pale green cones in summer, turning purple by autumn. The grey-green variety ***C.a.*** **'Glauca'** is more widely grown and more striking.

C. deodara DEODAR
Z: 6-7 H: 45 m (150 ft) F
Small glossy pointed leaves and pendulous habit. Generally lives for only 80 to 90 years in the UK.

C. libani CEDAR OF LEBANON
Z: 6-7 · H: 24·5-36 m (80-120 ft) M-F
Erect hardy tree with flattened horizontal layers of foliage, very dark green but sometimes grey. Handsome cones and impressive gnarled trunk.

CELTIS
C. occidentalis HACKBERRY, NETTLE TREE
Z: 4 H: 12 m (40 ft) S
Prefers a warm climate and will tolerate drought and pollution. Content with most soils and useful in larger town gardens because the branches are tough and the roots long enough not to uproot paving. The toothed green leaves explain the allusion to nettles and these turn pale yellow in autumn. Tiny purple berries in autumn may last through winter and the rough knobbled grey bark is an attractive feature.

CERCIDIPHYLLUM
C. japonicum KATSURA TREE
Z: 5 H: 15 m (50 ft) M
A Japanese tree which does best in a continental climate where it makes a good shade tree with its spreading branches of shiny heart-shaped leaves on a single trunk. Spring foliage has a red tinge, leaves becoming blue-green in summer then red or yellow before they drop. Dark brown bark which becomes shaggy with age while new branches are tipped with red. This lime-hater needs full sun and shelter from wind or frost.

CERCIS
C. canadensis REDBUD
Z: 6 H: 12 m (40 ft) S
A lovely flowering tree popular in the USA where the spring branches are smothered in purplish blossom. Foliage fresh green and heart-shaped. Tolerates all soils provided well drained.

C. siliquastrum JUDAS TREE
Z: 8 H: 9 m (30 ft) S
An excellent picturesque free-flowering small tree whose bare branches are hidden by purple-pink flowers in late spring. The green seed pods ripen with a red tinge in autumn. Prefers full sun and frost protection.

CHAMAECYPARIS
C. lawsoniana LAWSON CYPRESS
Z: 5 H: 30-36 m (100-120 ft) M
Makes a feathery pyramid of fresh green. Pink or red strobili and light-brown male cones in autumn. Innumerable varieties varying in leaf colour, foliage texture, branch configuration and many slower-growing sorts. The variety ***C.l.*** **'Wisellii'** is one of the most dramatic with grey foliage, an upright habit and fern-like branchlets.

C. obtusa HINOKI CYPRESS
Z: 3 H: 30-36 m (100-120 ft) S
An attractive conical shape of distinctive shiny dense green foliage. Green cones ripen to an orange-brown colour.

C. pisifera SAWARA CYPRESS
Z: 3 H: 30-36 m (100-120 ft) M
Makes a pyramid of upturned shiny green sprays of narrow foliage. Prolific small brown cones. Dislikes lime.

Cotinus coggygria **'Royal Purple'**

CHAMAEROPS

C. humilis EUROPEAN FAN PALM, DWARF FAN PALM

Z: 9 H: 6 m (20 ft) VS

Huge palmate leaves 1 m (3 ft) across on delicate stalks. Trunk roughly scarred. May produce small yellow flowers and round fruits depending on sex.

CITRUS

C. aurantifolia × fortunella LIMEQUAT

Z: 10 H: 6 m (20 ft) M

Dark green evergreen producing plenty of yellow, oval, tart fruits given a long warm summer. All citrus are very prone to scale insects and mealy bug, for which a constant search should be made, especially if they are grown in pots.

***C.* 'Aurantium'** SEVILLE ORANGE

Z: 10 H: 6 m (20 ft) M

Evergreen oval leaves, small fragrant white flowers and round bitter oranges, perfect for making marmalade.

C. limoni LEMON

Z: 9–10 H: 6 m (20 ft) M

Evergreen oval leaves have a crinkled edge. White flowers; fruits ripen only in warm, sunny climate.

C. reticulata TANGERINE, MANDARIN ORANGE

Z: 9 H: 6 m (20 ft) M

Makes a small spreading tree of narrow dark green leaves. Small sweet orange fruits. Hardier than the sweet orange, *C. sinensis*.

C. sinensis SWEET ORANGE

Z: 10 H: 6 m (20 ft) M

Shiny oval leaves, sweet-scented white flowers and large, round orange fruits, very sweet when ripe.

CLADRASTIS

C. lutea YELLOW-WOOD

Z: 3 H: 15–18 m (50–60 ft) (usually up to 15 m (50 ft) in UK) M

An excellent shade tree with fine late-season yellow colour to the foliage. Fragrant white flowers in summer, usually blooming in alternate years. Brown pods in autumn. Prefers full sun but will tolerate any soil providing it is rich and moist enough for the long roots.

CLETHRA

C. arborea LILY-OF-THE-VALLEY TREE

Z: 9 H: 6–7·5 m (20–25 ft) S

Small, dark green, evergreen tree with fragrant white flowers. Lime-hater requiring shelter and sun or partial shade.

COFFEA

C. arabica ARABIAN COFFEE

Z: 10 H: 6 m (20 ft) M

An interesting tender arboreal shrub with shiny evergreen foliage and white flowers in spring followed by red berries in summer.

CORDYLINE

C. australis CABBAGE TREE

Z: 8–9 H: 12 m (40 ft) S–M

Tender erect tree with close-foliaged head of evergreen leaves. Hanging clusters of small fragrant white flowers produce small blue-white berries.

CORNUS (see page 110)

CORYLUS

C. avellana HAZEL, COBNUT

Z: 4 H: 6 m (20 ft) M

More often a deciduous shrub. Mainly grown for pretty catkins and edible nuts in shaggy husks. Catkins appear in spring but foliage also colourful in autumn. A good small specimen tree because it is tough; also useful for screening. ***C.a.* 'Contorta'** Also known as CORKSCREW HAZEL. Spiral twigs. Catkins at their best in late winter.

***C. maxima* 'Purpurea'** PURPLE-LEAF FILBERT

Z: 5 H: 9 m (30 ft) M

Purple colour to catkins and foliage. Excellent for flower arranging.

COTINUS

C. coggygria SMOKE TREE, VENETIAN SUMACH

Z: 5 H: 4·5 m (15 ft) M

Fine autumn colours. Feathery flowers turn smoke grey. ***C.c.* 'Royal Purple'** Deep red purple colour to foliage during the summer.

C. obovatus (*C. americanus*)
AMERICAN SMOKE TREE
Z: 5 H: 9 m (30 ft) M
Sun-loving small tree or shrub with strong foliage, sometimes with a purple tinge and wonderful fire-red autumn colour. Prefers sun and tolerates drought.

COTONEASTER
***C.* 'Cornubia'**
Z: 6 H: 6-9 m (20-30 ft) F
A semi-evergreen with narrow pointed leaves and a mass of red berries in autumn.

***C.* 'Hybridus Pendulus'**
Z: 6 H: 6-12 m (20-40 ft) S-M
Weeping branches on an upright stem and plenty of red fruit set among small evergreen leaves makes this ideal for sites with limited space.

C. salicifolius
Z: 7 H: 6 m (20 ft) F
Tall evergreen with arching branches, slender leaves and lots of berries.

C.* × *watereri
Z: 7 H: 4·5 m (15 ft) F
Spreading semi-evergreen, small bright red berries.

+ ***CRATAEGOMESPILUS***
+ ***C. dardarii***
BRONVAUX MEDLAR
Z: 6 H: 4·5-6 m (15-20 ft) S
A hybrid naturally produced from a medlar grafted onto a hawthorn. It produces a golden autumn colour, fluffy white flower heads and fruits like small medlars of curiosity value; it makes a nice small tree. + ***C.d.* 'Jules d'Asnière'** Spiny branches and corymbs of white flowers.

CRATAEGUS (see page 114)

CRYPTOMERIA
C. japonica JAPANESE CEDAR
Z: 6 H: 45 m (150 ft) M-F
Tall narrow pyramid of evergreen foliage with pale yellow flowers in winter and dark brown cones. Prefers damp soil. ***C.j.* 'Elegans'** is a bushy tree with grey-blue summer foliage and bronze autumn and winter colour.

CUNNINGHAMIA
C. lanceolata CHINESE FIR
Z: 7 H: 18 m (60 ft) S-M
Bright green evergreen with oval cones.

× ***CUPRESSOCYPARIS***
× ***C. leylandii*** LEYLAND CYPRESS
Z: 6 H: 18 m (60 ft) F
Forms fairly narrow columns of dense dark green or grey foliage. Other forms may be golden. Vigorous evergreen useful for mixed screening; it can make 18 m (60 ft) in twenty-five years. Salt-resistant.

CUPRESSUS
C. arizonica (*C. glabra*)
SMOOTH ARIZONA CYPRESS
Z: 7 H: 14 m (45 ft) M
Pronounced conical shape with greyish foliage and interesting cones. Bark sometimes flaky and reddish.

C. macrocarpa MONTEREY CYPRESS
Z: 7-8 H: 18-27·5 m (60-90 ft) F
Useful conifer in coastal gardens for its tolerance to salt winds and exposure and for its rapid growth. May be frost tender. Cones have a purple tinge. Foliage has attractive scent and makes a fine spreading head. It is readily and cheaply produced from seed but transplants badly if not planted out early.

C. sempervirens ITALIAN CYPRESS
Z: 9 H: 24·5-45 m (80-150 ft) F
Dense dark green foliage and shiny green cones which later turn brown.

CYDONIA
C. oblonga COMMON QUINCE
Z: 6 H: 4·5-6 m (15-20 ft) S-M
Deciduous spreading tree with yellow autumn colour, white or pale pink spring blossom and pear-shaped, hard yellow fruits useful for tart jellies.

Cotoneaster* 'Cornubia'** ***Davidia involucrata (top)

Eucalyptus dalrympleana

Cytisus

C. battandieri

Z: 8–9 H: 4·5 m (15 ft) F

Yellow flowers in summer with fruity scent, long hairy pea pods. Leaves are covered with silver hairs. Does not really like lime or chalk. Prefers a sunny position.

Davidia

D. involucrata

HANDKERCHIEF TREE, DOVE TREE

Z: 6 H: 12 m (40 ft) M

An exotic round-headed specimen tree making a fine spring display of huge white leaves or bracts which flutter in the breeze. The true flower is enclosed in the white bract and is followed by green pear-shaped fruits. A hardy tree, it prefers light shade and rich moist soil.

Diospyros

D. kaki CHINESE PERSIMMON

Z: 8 H: 6–12 m (20–40 ft) S

A pretty deciduous fruit tree with glossy green oval leaves and large bright orange or yellow edible fruits. Prefers a sunny position and will tolerate drought.

D. virginiana COMMON PERSIMMON

Z: 5 H: 12–20 m (40–65 ft) M

More pendulous branches than *D. kaki*. Smaller fruits, edible after frost.

Drimys

D. winteri WINTER BARK

Z: 8 H: 6 m (20 ft) M

Small, large-leaved evergreen with greyish aromatic bark and sweet-scented white flowers in spring. Will not grow on chalk soils.

Elaeagnus

E. angustifolia OLEASTER, RUSSIAN OLIVE

Z: 3 H: 12 m (40 ft) M

A pretty silver-grey deciduous shrub or small tree with clusters of small fragrant silver-yellow flowers in early summer and sweet yellow berries in autumn, covered with silver scales and popular with birds. Needs sun but grows under most conditions, tolerating wind, pollution and drought, making it useful for town gardens and as a wind-break. Dislikes chalk.

Embothrium

E. coccineum CHILEAN FIREBUSH

Z: 8–9 H: 12 m (40 ft) S

An upright evergreen tree or shrub covered in glossy green foliage. Clusters of exotic orange-red flowers in early summer. Requires shade and a lime-free soil. ***E.c. longifolium*** Long-leaved fast-growing form with masses of orange-scarlet flowers.

Erica

E. arborea TREE HEATH

Z: 7 H: 4·5–6 m (15–20 ft) F

Tiny evergreen leaves make a rounded shape smothered in heavily-scented clusters of small white flowers in spring. Lime-hater which thrives on sandy soil.

Eriobotrya

E. japonica LOQUAT

Z: 8 H: 7·5 m (25 ft) M

Handsome evergreen with large leathery leaves. In mild conditions it will produce white scented flowers and edible yellow fruits. Prefers a sheltered position.

Eucalyptus

E. coccifera TASMANIAN SNOW GUM

Z: 6 H: 20 m (65 ft) M

Grey-green leaves, peppermint-scented when crushed, and whitish-grey bark that peels in long strips.

E. dalrympleana BROAD-LEAVED KINDLING BARK

Z: 8 H: 30 m (100 ft) F

Bark peels in large patches, pale cream when young, ageing to light-brown. Elegant but not hardy.

E. glaucescens TINGIRINGI GUM

Z: 7 H: 12 m (40 ft) M

Small tree with white fresh young bark, ageing to grey, and reddish-brown stems with a silvery bloom. Long, slender silvery leaves.

***Fagus sylvatica* 'Purpurea'** (right)

Fagus sylvatica

E. gunnii
Z: 7 H: 20 m (65 ft) M
Smooth greenish-grey bark, small elliptical waxy leaves and slender graceful habit.

E. niphophila SNOW GUM
Z: 7 H: 12 m (40 ft) M
A very attractive tree with glossy leaves that are mahogany coloured when newly opened and dark red young branches.

E. pauciflora
Z: 7 H: 20 m (65 ft) M
Several crooked stems, thick leathery leaves.

EUCOMMIA
E. ulmoides HARDY RUBBER TREE
Z: 5 H: 20 m (65 ft) M
Simple glossy leather leaves. Winged seeds on female trees. Drought-tolerant.

EUCRYPHIA
E. glutinosa
Z: 7–8 H: 7·5 m (25 ft) S
Slow-growing tree at its best in summer when even young specimens flower with a mass of white blossoms with yellow anthers. The green leaves have orange-red autumn colours. Prefers an acid soil and sun or light shade.

E. × nymansensis (*E. cordifolia × E. glutinosa*) **'Nymansay'**
Z: 7 H: 12 m (40 ft) S
Very popular evergreen producing an absolute mass of white when in flower. Probably the best sort to plant in the UK.

EUONYMUS
E. europaeus COMMON SPINDLE TREE
Z: 3 H: 6 m (20 ft) F
Mainly grown for its splendid red and orange autumn colour and its lobed fruit, whose pink-red shell splits open to show off the orange seeds. Foliage in summer is fresh green. The variety ***E.e.* 'Red Cascade'** is very free-fruiting. ***E.e.* 'Albus'** White berries. Looks good planted with red-berried form.

FAGUS

F. englerana
Z: 4 H: 15 m (50 ft) S
A good smaller beech tree which can be used with native trees for small copses.

F. sylvatica COMMON BEECH
Z: 5 H: 36 m (120 ft) M
Tolerates both very acid and alkaline soils, has reddish autumn colour and pleasant smooth bark. ***F.s.* 'Asplenifolia'** has attractive finely cut leaves and is slower growing than most. ***F.s.* 'Dawyck'** Fastigiate variety. ***F.s.* 'Pendula'** A very slow-growing weeping form with silver-grey bark; it rarely makes more than about 15 m (50 ft). ***F.s.* 'Purpurea'** The Purple Beech whose pale red spring foliage turns dark purple as it matures. ***F.s.* 'Riversii'** Another purple form.

FATSIA

F. japonica FALSE CASTOR OIL PALM
Z: 8 H: 4·5 m (15 ft) M
An exotic plant which remains evergreen unless the winter is particularly hard. The large glossy hand-shaped leaves are brightened by small starry white flowers borne in large numbers on huge panicles in autumn. Prefers full sun and plenty of moisture but will tolerate some shade, chalky soils, pollution and coastal sites.

FICUS

F. carica COMMON FIG
Z: 6–8 H: 9 m (30 ft) F
A handsome fast-growing tree with wide-spreading shady branches. The bark is smooth and grey and the edible fruits anything from yellowish-green to brown or purple. Trees will start to bear fruit from four years after planting and they prefer a sunny sheltered position – maybe against a warm wall. Restricting the roots encourages fruiting.

FORTUNELLA

F. margarita KUMQUAT
Z: 9 H: 3 m (10 ft) S
White flowers among dark green evergreen leaves in spring and oval pale orange edible fruits with a slightly bitter taste.

FOTHERGILLA

F. major (*F. monticola*)
Z: 6 H: 3·5 m (10 ft) M
A rounded bushy tree with waxy dark glossy green leaves that turn yellow, coppery-brown or red in autumn, and scented yellow flower spikes on bare branches in spring. Best grown in light, peaty soil in full sun.

FRANKLINIA

F. alatamaha FRAKLIN TREE
Z: 6 H: 6 m (20 ft) M
Can be frost-tender unless the summer is hot and ripens the new growth. Dark green glossy leaves turn red in autumn. Flowers in late summer are white, waxy and fragrant.

FRAXINUS (see page 116)

GARRYA

G. elliptica SILK TASSEL BUSH
Z: 7 H: 4·5 m (15 ft) M
Grown for its spectacular winter display of long, grey-green catkins against the deep evergreen leaves. Prefers a little shelter and well-drained soil. Will tolerate chalk soils, some shade and/or a coastal site.

GENISTA

G. aetnensis MOUNT ETNA BROOM
Z: 8 H: 6 m (20 ft) S-M
A sun-lover with spiky slender leaves and masses of yellow pea-flowers in summer. Will tolerate chalk.

GINKGO

G. biloba MAIDENHAIR TREE
Z: 5 H: 24·5 m (80 ft) S
Wonderful spreading shade tree with unusual fan-shaped bright green leaves which develop yellow borders in autumn. The round yellow seeds smell horrid if split open. They only occur on female trees and where there are males to pollinate them. Lime- and pollution-tolerant but rather large.

Franklinia alatamaha

Fothergilla major

GLEDITSIA
G. triacanthos HONEY LOCUST
Z: 5 H: 42 m (140 ft) M
Attractive glossy green pinnate leaves like fern fronds on spiny trunk and branches. A pretty light shade tree with yellow autumn colour. It produces large brown crinkled pods 30 cm (12 in) long and 2.5 cm (1 in) wide. Tolerates chalk.
***G.t.* 'Columnaris'** Columnar form.
***G.t.* 'Moraine'** Thornless form with wide-spreading branches and attractive yellow-green, bell-shaped flowers. Grows on most soils. Drought-tolerant.
***G.t.* 'Sunburst'** A smaller form – growing to about 6-9 m (20-30 ft). Thornless and the young foliage is bright yellow.

GRISELINIA
G. littoralis
Z: 5 H: 18 m (60 ft) M
Glossy yellow or yellow-green evergreen leaves. It is good in coastal areas and some forms are thought to be hardier than others.

HALESIA
H. carolina SNOWDROP TREE, SILVER BELL
Z: 7 H: 10·5 m (35 ft) F; UK 6-9 m (20-30 ft) F
Clusters of flowers like white snowdrops. Scaly bark. Prefers sun and needs a sheltered position and moist well-drained soil.

H. monticola
MOUNTAIN SNOWDROP TREE, MOUNTAIN SILVERBELL
Z: 7 H: 18 m (60 ft) F
Pyramid of white flowers in spring. Foliage yellow in autumn. Can be grown in part shade.

HAMAMELIS (see page 118)

HEBE
H. salicifolia
Z: 8 H: 3·5-4·5 m (12-15 ft) F
Tender shrub producing long spikes of thickly crowded white flowers in late summer. Tolerates dry chalky soil and coastal conditions. Prefers a warm sheltered spot. Fine evergreen foliage.

HIBISCUS
H. syriacus
Z: 5 H: 3 m (10 ft) S
An upright bush of green leaves; several varieties with pink, white or mauve single or double flowers with red markings in late summer/autumn. Needs a warm sheltered spot but will tolerate dry chalky soil and coastal conditions. Cut it back hard each spring to keep it compact.

HOHERIA
H. glabrata (*H. lyallii*)
Z: 8 H: 4·5 m (15 ft) M
Rather tender but worth growing for its dense show of scented white flowers in summer against the oval, green leaves. Prefers sun and shelter but will tolerate chalky soil and coastal positions.

H. sexstylosa
Z: 8-9 H: 6 m (20 ft) M
Glossy light green semi-evergreen leaves and white flowers in August.

ILEX (see page 120)

JACARANDA
J. acutifolia JACARANDA
Z: 9 H: 15 m (50 ft) M-F
Fine feathery foliage and a mass of blue flowers. Requires a very sunny, dry position.

JUGLANS
J. cinerea BUTTERNUT
Z: 3 H: 18 m (60 ft) M
Wide-spreading deciduous tree with hanging catkins and pointed nut husks covered in sticky hairs.

J. nigra EASTERN BLACK WALNUT
Z: 4 H: 30 m (100 ft) M
Good, if rather large, shade-casting tree with spreading branches of long leaves and round shape. The timber is excellent.

Gleditsia triacanthos **'Sunburst'**

J. regia ENGLISH, COMMON or PERSIAN WALNUT
Z: 6 H: 18–30 m (60–100 ft) M
Deep shady spread of pinnate leaves; edible nuts in a hard round shell. Needs full sun and deep soil for the long roots. Unripe soft fruits can be pickled.

JUNIPERUS
J. chinensis CHINESE JUNIPER
Z: 4 H: 9 m (30 ft) S
A conical evergreen with dark green prickly leaves and green cones which turn purple ***J.c.* 'Aurea'** A bright golden form. Both have pretty yellow spring flowers.

J. virginiana PENCIL CEDAR, EASTERN RED CEDAR
Z: 2 H: 18 m (60 ft) S
Conical arrangement of tiny leaves on top of a long trunk. Cones ripen in the first year like small purplish berries. Peeling bark.

KALOPANAX
K. pictus CASTOR ARALIA
Z: 5 H: 15 m (50 ft) S
Large-leaved, shade tree that tolerates alkaline soil. The grey-green leaves have red autumn colour and in late summer are lightened by small white flowers which may produce tiny black berries. Prefers full sun and needs good soil.

KOELREUTERIA
K. paniculata GOLDEN RAIN TREE
Z: 7 H: 12 m (40 ft) S
Grown for its mass of yellow flower spikes in summer which make a spectacular display both on the tree and below it after they have fallen. The pinnate deciduous leaves start reddish in spring, turn blue-green and then, in autumn, yellow. Requires plenty of sun. Drought-tolerant.

LABURNUM
L. alpinum SCOTCH LABURNUM
Z: 5 H: 7·5 m (25 ft) M
A hardy tree with shiny leaves and large flower clusters. Tolerates most soils and pollution. ***L.a.* 'Aureum'** Golden foliage. Seed pods are highly poisonous.

***Laburnum* × *watereri* 'Vossii'**

L. anagyroides COMMON LABURNUM
Z: 5 H: 7·5–9 m (25–30 ft) M
Dull-green three-lobed leaves and drooping racemes of bright yellow flowers.

***L.* × *watereri* 'Vossii'**
Z: 6 H: 9 m (30 ft) M
One of the commonest laburnums in gardens, producing a waterfall of extra long racemes of golden flowers.

LAGERSTROEMIA
L. indica CRAPE MYRTLE
Z: 7 H: 6–9 m (20–30 ft) S
Small decorative tree with little dark green leaves and spikes of pink or red flowers from summer to autumn. The stems of older plants are very attractive. Pollution-tolerant. It needs very hot summers to flower well.

LARIX
L. decidua EUROPEAN LARCH, COMMON LARCH
Z: 3 H: 36 m (120 ft) F
Narrow conical shape with light green young leaves in spring turning dark green and then gold in autumn. Does not like chalk. Attractive red flowers and light brown cones.

Liquidambar styraciflua

Ligustrum ovalifolium

L. kaempferi JAPANESE LARCH
Z: 4 H: 30 m (100 ft) F
Grown for its young red or purple shoots with long green needles. Foliage turns yellow then orange in the autumn. Attractive cones.

L. laricina EASTERN LARCH, AMERICAN LARCH, TAMARACK
Z: 2 H: 15-24·5 m (50-80 ft) F
Pyramid of bright bluish foliage turning yellow in autumn. Reddish bark. Tolerates wet soil.

LAURUS
L. nobilis SWEET BAY, LAUREL
Z: 7 H: 10·5 m (35 ft) (occasionally up to 18 m (60 ft)) S
Makes dense pyramid shape of evergreen oval spicy dark green leaves, but is more often clipped into lollipop or hedge shapes. Needs protection from strong cold winds. ***L.n.*** **'Aurea'** Golden-leaved form.

LEPTOSPERMUM
L. scoparium MANUKA
Z: 9 H: 4·5 m (15 ft) M
Small-leaved evergreen with white flowers in spring and pea-sized fruits. ***L.s.*** **'Chapmanii'** Rosy-red flowers and bronze-coloured leaves.

LIGUSTRUM
L. lucidum CHINESE PRIVET
Z: 7 H: 9-15 m (30-50 ft) F
The glossy dark evergreen leaves of this dense shrub or tree are frequently clipped into formal shapes. Flowers are small and white in late summer; produces small blue-black berries about a month later. Likes sun but will tolerate shade. Requires some shelter. ***L.l.*** **'Tricolor'** An upright, variegated form showing white and pink.

L. ovalifolium
Z: 6 H: 4·5 m (15 ft) F
Popular but not very interesting evergreen, good for clipping. Will tolerate chalk or clay. ***L.o.*** **'Aureum'** is a more interesting golden form which, if allowed to grow on as an unpruned tree, looks rather striking.

LIQUIDAMBAR
L. styraciflua SWEET GUM
Z: 5 H: 21 m (70 ft) M
Attractive domed deciduous tree with neat branches of maple-shaped leaves and good autumn colour lasting for several weeks. A good specimen tree in the town garden in moist soil and a sunny position. Will also grow close to water or in coastal areas if sheltered from wind. Produces unusual prickly brown seed-cases in autumn. Dislikes chalky soil and frost. ***L.s.*** **'Aurea'** Leaves speckled with yellow.

LIRIODENDRON
L. chinense CHINESE TULIP TREE
Z: 5 H: 15 m (50 ft) S
Rare in Europe, similar to *L. tulipifera* with yellow autumn colour and smaller flowers. The summer foliage has glaucous undersides. Needs some shelter from cold winds.

L. tulipifera TULIP TREE
Z: 5 H: 30 m (100 ft) F
Large shiny green leaves turning rich yellow in autumn and yellow-green tulip-shaped flowers among the dense domed mass of foliage in summer. Thrives in a moist soil. ***L.t.*** **'Aureo-marginatum'** Leaves edged with yellow. ***L.t.*** **'Fastigiatum'** More erect, columnar form.

MAGNOLIA (see page 122)

MALUS (see page 126)

MESPILUS
M. germanica MEDLAR
Z: 4 H: 4·5 m (15 ft) M
Useful shade or specimen tree with attractive spreading branches and russet autumn colour. The late-spring blossom is pink or white and is followed by hard brown fruits which are edible once they have softened and are best used for jelly. Requires a sunny position and rich soil.

Myrtus luma

METASEQUOIA

M. glyptostroboides DAWN REDWOOD, WATER FIR, SHUI-HSA

Z: 5 H: 30-36 m (100-120 ft) M

One of the oldest species in existence – but only discovered in 1947 – this is a popular deciduous conifer grown for its pollution resistance and hardiness. Makes a shaggy spreading pyramid of pale green foliage which turns reddish-pink and then bronze by autumn. A hot summer may produce dark brown cones. Bark is dark grey, branches turn brown. Prefers full sun and moist soil although it will tolerate some chalk in the soil.

METROSIDEROS

M. robusta

Z: 9 H: 12 m (40 ft) S

New shoots have a red tinge and late summer flowers are bright red among the dark green, leathery foliage of this tender evergreen. A lime-hater.

MORUS

M. alba WHITE MULBERRY

Z: 5 H: 13·5 m (45 ft) M-F

Dense shade tree of heart-shaped leaves. White or pink fruit can be acidic. Will grow in full sun or light shade on any soil including alkaline types. Has long roots and mature specimens are drought-tolerant. Hardy and tolerant of urban and coastal conditions.

M. nigra BLACK MULBERRY, COMMON MULBERRY

Z: 5 H: 9 m (30 ft) S

Juicy purplish-red edible berries in great numbers among the glossy green, wide-spreading foliage. Mature specimens have attractive gnarled trunks and branches.

MYRTUS

M. luma (*Myrceugenia apiculata*) MYRTLE

Z: 9 H: 6 m (20 ft) but 18 m (60 ft) in warmer climates S-M

Evergreen with small oval leaves, white flowers in summer and small black/

Nyssa sylvatica

Parrotia persica

purple edible fruits. Peeling cinnamon-coloured bark is particularly attractive. Lime-tolerant.

NOTHOFAGUS

N. antarctica ANTARCTIC BEECH, NIRRE
Z: 8 H: 15 m (50 ft) M
Imposing tree with dark green glossy leaves often supported by many stems and spreading branches. Needs shelter from wind and prefers neutral soil.

N. procera RAULI
Z: 8 H: 24·5 m (80 ft) VF
Lighter green, almost yellow foliage with attractive veining and good autumn colour. Prominent buds.

NYSSA

N. sylvatica BLACK GUM, SOUR GUM, TUPELO
Z: 5 H: 30 m (100 ft) S
Shiny green leaves turn bright red or orange in autumn and even the stalks look red. Blue-black seeds in autumn. Hardy but prefers full sun and moist acid soil. Will tolerate light shade but is difficult to transplant, so plant young.

OLEA

O. europaea COMMON OLIVE
Z: 9 H: 4·5-9 m (15-30 ft) S
Shiny evergreen leaves look silver below. Small fragrant white flowers in late summer produce green, later purple, olives in warm climates. Tender but will tolerate drought.

OXYDENDRUM

O. arboreum SORREL TREE
Z: 5 H: 6 m (20 ft) S
A domed head of narrow green leaves on top of a slender trunk. Foliage turns red in autumn. Small white flowers on 15-25-cm (6-10-in) spikes in summer. Soil must be lime-free.

PARROTIA

P. persica IRONWOOD
Z: 6 H: 12 m (40 ft) S
Wide-spreading tree valued for its autumn foliage when the shiny dark green leaves turn red, yellow, orange and pink. The flowers in early spring are out before the leaves and have interesting red stamens; the resultant seeds are brown. Grows well in cooler climates but is most colourful in full sun. Prefers acid soil but will tolerate lime. Branches come low to the ground – lop these off if you want to enjoy the flaking bark in winter. There is a weeping cultivar with even better colour.

PAULOWNIA

P. fargesii (*P. lilacina*)
Z: 6-8 H: 20 m (65 ft) M-F
A spread of large deciduous leaves and, this tree's most outstanding virtue, scented spikes of blue-purple and cream foxglove-like flowers in spring. Needs sun and shelter. Young trees do not flower so be prepared to wait.

P. tomentosa EMPRESS TREE
Z: 6-8 H: 15 m (50 ft) M-F
Spring flowers sweet-scented with a yellow stripe, followed by seed pods.

PHILLYREA

P. latifolia
Z: 6 H: 9 m (30 ft) S
Shrub or tree with dense spread of branches. Shiny dark green leaves are evergreen, flowers small and greenish-white and fruits like blue-black berries.

PHOTINIA

P. × fraseri
Z: 8 H: 3·6 m (12 ft) F
Evergreen leaves are bronze when young, turning to a glossy dark green. The variety ***P. × f.* 'Red Robin'** has brilliant red young leaves.

P. serrulata
Z: 7 H: 12 m (40 ft) M
An evergreen with shiny dark green leaves but young foliage is coppery-red and the flowers in spring are white. Small red berries appear in autumn and early winter. Lime-tolerant and enjoys a position in sunshine.

Paulownia tomentosa

***Picea pungens* 'Glauca'** (top)
Pyrus communis

PICEA

P. abies NORWAY or COMMON SPRUCE
Z: 2 H: 36 m (120 ft) M-F
A narrow column of green needles producing pinkish strobili on more mature specimens and large cones. Many varieties, some no more than small shrubs.

P. omorika SERBIAN SPRUCE
Z: 4 H: 30 m (100 ft) M
Narrow elegant cone of uptilted grey-green needles and a remarkably slender trunk. Oval cones. Frost- and pollution-resistant. Tolerates most soils.

P. pungens COLORADO or BLUE SPRUCE
Z: 3 H: 24·5-30 m (80-100 ft) M
Greenish-blue colour and strong pyramidal shape. Long narrow cones.

PINUS (see page 128)

PITTOSPORUM

P. tenuifolium KOHUHU
Z: 8 H: 9 m (30 ft) M
Twigs are dark, nearly black and the evergreen foliage grey-tinted with a crinkled look. Dark chocolate-purple spring flowers have a sweet scent and the fruits ripen to black. Small and bushy like a shrub.

P. tobira TOBIRA
Z: 8-9 H: 6 m (20 ft) M
Evergreen bushy tree with glossy green leaves and cream sweet-scented summer flowers. Will resist drought.

PLATANUS

P. × acerifolia LONDON PLANE
Z: 6 H: 42 m (140 ft) F
Large tree usually grown for its pollution resistance. Leaves are large and lobed making a spreading dome of foliage. Attractive flaky bark.

P. occidentalis SYCAMORE, BUTTONWOOD, WESTERN PLANE
Z: 5 H: 45 m (150 ft) F
Attractive peeling white bark and interesting bristly fruits.

PONCIRUS

P. trifoliata JAPANESE BITTER ORANGE
Z: 7 H: 4·5 m (15 ft) S
Small tree with attractive leaves on spiny stems, scented white blossom producing small, downy, edible but distinctly bitter 'oranges'.

POPULUS

P. alba WHITE POPLAR, ABELE
Z: 4 H: 30 m (100 ft) F
Hardy spreading tree with attractive light foliage and fine bark. With all poplars, roots may cause problems to drains and paving, but quick to establish and tolerant of most conditions including salt and pollution.

P. balsamifera BALSAM POPLAR
Z: 2 H: 30 m (100 ft) F
Pungent scent to stems and leaves. Interesting winter buds covered with sticky yellow resin are also scented. Dislikes chalky soil.

***P. × canadensis* 'Serotina Aurea'**
Z: 2 H: 30 m (100 ft) F
Rich yellow foliage in both spring and autumn.

P. × candicans BALM OF GILEAD, ONTARIO POPLAR
Z: 7 H: 30 m (100 ft) F
Foliage light-coloured below and emits a balsam scent. Good shade tree. ***P. × c.* 'Aurora'** A variegated cultivar with white and pink tints to the foliage.

P. lasiocarpa CHINESE POPLAR
Z: 5 H: 18 m (60 ft) S
The heart-shaped leaves are the largest of the genus, young foliage having red markings. Attractive catkins.

***P. nigra* 'Italica'** LOMBARDY POPLAR
Z: 3 H: 27·5 m (90 ft) F
Narrow erect form producing interesting catkins.

P. tremula ASPEN
Z: 3 H: 15 m (50 ft) F
Young foliage is woolly becoming

smooth with a grey colour, turning yellow in autumn. Leaves tend to flutter or shiver in the wind.

PRUNUS (see page 130)

PSEUDOLARIX
P. amabilis GOLDEN LARCH
Z: 5-6 H: 27·5 m (90 ft) S
Similar to the true larch but with larger leaves. A lime-hater with lovely golden autumn colour.

PTELEA
P. trifoliata HOP TREE
Z: 4 H: 7·5 m (25 ft) S
Makes a round-headed tree with shiny foliage, small greenish-white fragrant flowers in summer and green winged seeds. Enjoys light shade.

PTEROCARYA
P. fraxinifolia CAUCASIAN WINGNUT
Z: 6 H: 30 m (100 ft) F
The name comes from the hanging bunches of winged seeds, green in summer turning brown in autumn. Wide-spreading branches of shiny deciduous leaves. Prefers moist soil and full sun.

PYRUS
P. calleryana **'Chanticleer'**
Z: 5 H: 15 m (50 ft) F
Cultivar of the Chinese Wild Pear with narrow conical crown. The glossy leaves turn rich purple and claret in autumn.

P. communis COMMON PEAR
Z: 5 H: 9-12 m (30-40 ft) M
Good reddish autumn colour, mass of blossom and large sweet edible fruits. Likes a sunny position.

P. salicifolia **'Pendula'**
WEEPING SILVER PEAR
Z: 5 H: 7·5 m (25 ft) M
Most attractive specimen tree with delicate weeping branches of narrow silver foliage.

QUERCUS (see page 134)

RHODODENDRON (see page 136)

RHUS
R. typhina STAG'S HORN SUMACH
Z: 4 H: 10·5 m (35 ft) M
Attractive pinnate foliage, turning rich orange and purple in autumn. Clusters of yellow-green or red flowers (according to sex) in summer. Red furry fruits in autumn. Thrives in full sun and is pollution-tolerant. ***R.t.*** **'Dissecta'** (Z: 3 H: 6 m/20 ft) A female cultivar with fern-like foliage and good autumn colour.

ROBINIA (see page 138)

SALIX
S. alba WHITE WILLOW
Z: 2 H: 27·5 m (90 ft) S
Upright tree with downy white foliage which turns yellow in autumn. Will not thrive on chalk. Like all willows, the branches are slender and graceful and the roots can be invasive, preferring damp soil. ***S.a.*** **'Chermesina'** Also known as the SCARLET WILLOW. Red-orange bark outstanding in winter. This form grows to about 15 m (50 ft). ***S.a.*** **'Vitellina'** Also known as the GOLDEN STEMMED WILLOW. Another small form with bright yellow shoots.

S. babylonica WEEPING WILLOW
Z: 7 H: 12 m (40 ft) F
The classic weeping shape associated with willows – drooping branches of narrow leaves and spring flowers. Frequently seen beside water.

S. caprea **'Pendula'**
Z: 4 H: 4.5 m (15 ft) F
Weeping form of the Goat Willow which has downy foliage and large yellow catkins.

S. × chrysocoma
GOLDEN WEEPING WILLOW
Z: 2 H: 12 m (40 ft) F
It has a wide-spreading habit and is usually wrongly planted in town gardens, too near the house, with in-

Rhus typhina
(female flower)

Rhus typhina (below)

Pyrus salicifolia
'Pendula' (bottom)

Stewartia pseudocamellia

Taxodium distichum

sufficient room. It must be at least 18–24.5 m (60–80 ft) from the house unless there is a permanent high water table. Its branches are very brittle and the tree is liable to wind damage. It is also very susceptible to the disease Anthracnose.

S. daphnoides VIOLET WILLOW
Z: 5 H: 12 m (40 ft) M
More upright form with shiny dark green leaves, dark purple stems, white blossom and striking catkins.

***S. matsudana* 'Tortuosa'**
CORKSCREW WILLOW,
DRAGON'S CLAW WILLOW
Z: 5 H: 12 m (40 ft) F
Curiously twisted branches and smooth, bright green foliage. Spring flowers.

***S. purpurea* 'Pendula'**
Z: 4 H: 3 m (10 ft) F
Weeping form with purple-tinged new foliage, leaves vivid blue-white underneath. Thrives in dryish ground better than most willows.

SAMBUCUS
S. canadensis
Z: 4 H: 4·5 m (15 ft) F
Bushy large shrub from north-eastern America, similar to the Common Elder. ***S.c.* 'Maxima'** Long leaves and large flower clusters.

S. nigra COMMON ELDER
Z: 6 H: 9 m (30 ft) F
Shrub or tree with large flat heads of small white fragrant flowers in summer followed by bunches of shiny black edible berries. Chalk and shade tolerant. The variegated, cut-leaved and purple forms are better subjects for gardens. ***S.n.* 'Aurea'** Yellow leaves. ***S.n.* 'Laciniata'** Parsley-like leaves.

S. racemosa RED-BERRIED ELDER
Z: 4 H: 4·5 m (15 ft) F
Less vigorous shrubby elder with attractive red berries. ***S.r.* 'Plumosa Aurea'** is a yellow form with bright golden foliage.

SASSAFRAS
S. albidum SASSAFRAS
Z: 9 H: 27·5 m (90 ft) M
Interesting blue-black fruits against bright green foliage. An aromatic tree which likes a warm aspect and lime-free soil. Not suitable for the UK.

SCIADOPITYS
S. verticillata
JAPANESE UMBRELLA PINE
Z: 6 H: 15-23 m (50–75 ft) S
Canopy of glossy green foliage on top of a long trunk with attractive red-brown peeling bark. Interesting cones. Prefers a damp lime-free soil.

SEQUOIA
S. sempervirens
COASTAL REDWOOD
Z: 6 H: 30 m (100 ft +) F
Spectacular tall tree with bright reddish bark and small red-brown cones. Tolerates most soils but will not thrive on an exposed site. It is easily increased by root shoots.

SEQUOIADENDRON
S. giganteum BIG TREE,
WELLINGTONIA, SIERRA REDWOOD
Z: 6 H: 45 m (150 ft) F
Perfectly hardy in the UK but less shade-tolerant than the Coastal Redwood. As it grows so tall it is only suitable for very large gardens. Reputed to be the tallest tree in the world.

SOPHORA
S. japonica JAPANESE PAGODA TREE
Z: 5 H: 15-24·5 m (50–80 ft) F
Pretty feathery foliage carried in a dense canopy making this an attractive shade or specimen tree for a site with plenty of sun and a moist deep soil for the tree's long roots. Mature trees may flower in late summer/early autumn in creamy-white clusters, followed by yellow pods through winter. Pollution-tolerant. The variety ***S.j.* 'Pendula'** at up to 4.5 m (15 ft) makes an attractive small specimen tree for a lawn.

Topiary with lilacs

S. tetraptera NEW ZEALAND SOPHORA, KOWHAI
Z: 8 H: 12 m (40 ft) S
Delicate green foliage and golden-yellow flowers in spring.

SORBUS (see page 140)

STEWARTIA
S. pseudocamellia (*Stuartia pseudo-camellia*) JAPANESE STEWARTIA
Z: 6 H: 20 m (65 ft) S
An ornamental flowering tree making an attractive canopy of foliage with white camellia-like flowers with gold centres, in succession from late summer to autumn. Red and yellow autumn colour to the foliage and flaking bark as tree matures. Prefers light shade and lime-free soil. Will not thrive in cold.

STRANVAESIA
S. davidiana (*Photinia davidiana*)
Z: 7 H: 10·5 m (35 ft) F
Evergreen shrub or small tree with white flowers in midsummer and an attractive display in autumn of bright red fruits. Many of its leaves have red autumn tints before they fall.

STYRAX
S. japonica SNOWBELL
Z: 5 H: 3–7·5 m (10–25 ft) S
An attractive small flowering tree with a wide spread of shiny leaves which turn red or yellow in autumn. The white flowers with yellow stamens in early summer are delicately scented and look particularly good from below, making this a good shade tree for a seating area. Hardy but prefers full sun or light shade.

S. obassia FRAGRANT SNOWBELL
Z: 6 H: 6–9 m (20–30 ft) M
Flowers bell-shaped and scented.

SYCOPSIS
S. sinensis
Z: 8 H: 6 m (20 ft) M
Bushy shrub with dark green, leathery evergreen leaves. Flowers enclosed in reddish-brown bracts and have yellow-orange anthers.

SYRINGA
S. oblata LILAC
Z: 5 H: 3·5 m (12 ft) M
Heart-shaped leaves, pale lilac flowers in spring and good red autumn colour. Young growth is susceptible to spring frosts. Not really hardy in the UK as it needs a harder and more settled winter.

S. reflexa
Z: 5 H: 4·5 m (15 ft) M
Dense cylindrical flowers in summer, purplish-pink outside and whitish inside. Reliably hardy.

S. vulgaris COMMON LILAC
Z: 4 H: 6 m (20 ft) F
A hardy plant grown for its deliciously scented mauve racemes of flowers in late spring. Tolerates chalky soils and likes plenty of sunshine but will grow in colder climates. The species tends to be suckerous but the various hybrid forms of garden lilac, with single and double flowers from white to yellow and deep red, are best propagated by cuttings.

TAMARIX
T. ramosissima (*T. pentandra*) TAMARISK
Z: 6 H: 6 m (20 ft) F
A lovely mass of grey-green foliage and, in spring or late summer, feathery spikes of pink flowers. Its delicate appearance belies its toughness and although it enjoys sun, it will tolerate a coastal site, both clay and chalky soil, and arid areas.

T. tetrandra
Z: 5 H: 4·5 m (15 ft) F
Striking black bark and feathery foliage; light pink flowers in spring.

TAXODIUM
T. ascendens POND CYPRESS, UPLAND CYPRESS
Z: 6 H: 21·5–24·5 m (70–80 ft) M
Bronze autumn colour and purple-tinted cones. Makes a narrow conical shape. Likes plenty of sun.

T. distichum SWAMP CYPRESS,
Z: 5 H: 30–36 m (100–120 ft) M
Tall yellow-green pyramid with roundish cones. Enjoys moist, even boggy soil where it throws up interesting aerial roots or 'knees'. Dislikes chalk.

Thuja occidentalis

Ulmus glabra **'Pendula'**

TAXUS

T. baccata COMMON YEW
Z: 6 H: 18 m (60 ft) S-M
Makes a broad conical tree becoming many-stemmed and strangely shaped with age. Small dark green foliage for clipping into geometric shapes or topiary forms. Red-coated seeds with green centres look like stuffed olives with colours reversed. Long-lived. Requires well-drained soil. Chalk- and drought-tolerant. There are many varietal forms.

T. cuspidata JAPANESE YEW
Z: 5 H: 15 m (50 ft) S
Attractive bark which becomes red-brown with age and golden undersides to foliage.

THUJA

T. occidentalis WHITE CEDAR, ARBOR VITAE
Z: 2 H: 18 m (60 ft) M
Makes a tall column of dull green apple-scented foliage. Grows on most soils.

T. plicata WESTERN RED CEDAR
Z: 5 H: 36 m (120 ft) M-F
Large dense spreading tree with reddish bark and green, later brown, cones. Foliage bright green and aromatic. Chalk- and shade-tolerant.

TILIA

T. americana LINDEN, AMERICAN LIME, AMERICAN BASSWOOD
Z: 3 H: 41 m (135 ft) F
Very big tree with fresh green foliage and fragrant clusters of creamy-white flowers in early summer. Sometimes grown to make a fragrant walkway.

T. mongolica MONGOLIAN LIME
Z: 4 H: 10·5-18 m (35-60 ft) S
The only lime you could possibly grow in small gardens but it is difficult to find. Its foliage is unusual – rather like birch.

***T.* 'Petiolaris'** WEEPING SILVER LIME
Z: 6 H: 30 m (100 ft) F
Dark green foliage has downy silver undersides. Blossom strongly scented in summer and toxic to bees. Slightly weeping habit.

TRACHYCARPUS

T. fortunei CHUSAN PALM, CHINESE WINDMILL PALM
Z: 8 H: 12 m (40 ft) S
Exotic-looking tree with a fibrous trunk and dark green palmate leaves above. Fragrant yellow flowers are small but very numerous. Small blue-black fruits.

TROCHODENDRON

T. aralioides
Z: 8 H: 9 m (30 ft) S
Lustrous evergreen leaves and vivid green flowers in late spring to early summer. Needs protection from winter winds.

TSUGA

T. canadensis CANADIAN HEMLOCK
Z: 4 H: 30 m (100 ft) M-F
Interesting dark red-brown bark. Makes a pyramid of evergreen needles and small pendulous cones. Will tolerate shade and any soil. Can be used for hedging.

T. heterophylla WESTERN HEMLOCK
Z: 4 H: 45 m (150 ft) M-F
Large conical tree with shiny dark green leaves and a mass of brown cones. Does not like chalky soil.

ULMUS

U. carpinifolia SMOOTH-LEAVED ELM, EUROPEAN FIELD ELM
Z: 5 H: 33 m (110 ft) F
Dramatic large tree with smooth narrow leaves, which thrives in full sun. Subject to Dutch Elm disease.

***U. glabra* 'Pendula'** TABLE TOP ELM
Z: 5 H: 9 m (30 ft) S
Small weeping form of the Wych Elm which has a flat top of dull green foliage. The flowers in early spring are quickly followed by furry fruits.

U. parvifolia CHINESE ELM
Z: 5 H: 18 m (60 ft) M
An elegant tree with tiny pointed leaves.

Tilia sp.

Taxus baccata (right)

Attractive mottled red-brown bark and greenish-white flowers from late summer to early autumn. Resistant to Dutch Elm disease.

VIBURNUM

V.* × *bodnantense

Z: 6 H: 3·6 m (12 ft) M

Usually grown for its spectacular autumn colour and delightfully fragrant pink or white flowers in autumn and early spring. Bright red fruits.

V. lanata WAYFARING TREE

Z: 4 H: 3·6–4·5 m (12–15 ft) M

Small tree or shrub with broad leaves and crimson autumn colour. Spring flowers are creamy-white; late summer fruits are red, quickly turning black. Chalk-tolerant

V. opulus GUELDER ROSE

Z: 3 H: 4·5 m (15 ft) F

More of a spreading shrub with maple-like leaves and white flowers in summer. Small red currant-like berries in autumn which may last through winter. Tolerates damp conditions and chalk.

VITEX

V. agnus-castus CHASTE TREE

Z: 7–8 H: 3–6 m (10–20 ft) M

A pungent scented tree with narrow leaflets and fragrant flowers in autumn. Good grown against a wall. Prune to keep it compact.

ZELKOVA

Z. carpinifolia ELM ZELKOVA

Z: 6 H: 30 m (100 ft) S

Very like an elm with a dense head of foliage and a smooth, later flaking, bark. Shade-tolerant. A long-lived and picturesque tree.

Z. serrata JAPANESE ZELKOVA

Z: 5 H: 30 m (100 ft) F

Short trunk with dense head of dark green foliage above which often fades to a good red or orange colour in autumn. Slightly susceptible to Dutch Elm disease.

—V—

THE CARE OF THE TREE

For the busy gardener, trees are ideal since they require relatively little attention, but because they are such a major feature in the garden landscape it is important that they look good at all times. In this chapter, we explain how a tree grows naturally, how to choose the right size and type of stock to plant, how to plant trees and keep them in good condition, including watering, fertilizing and pruning, how to maintain trees in pots in good condition, and the pests and diseases to watch out for and treat. Also included are lists of some of the best trees for particular purposes or effects – among them trees for spring or summer blossom, trees with good autumn foliage colour and useful evergreens.

*A venerable beech (*Fagus sylvatica*) in early autumn*

How a Tree Grows

It is worth knowing something about how a tree grows, so that you do not make basic mistakes in planting and growing the trees in your garden. The following is a very brief outline of the way a tree develops and grows.

In the wild, trees, like many other plants, self seed. Each seed is a remarkable package containing a living embryo and reserves of dried food. It will germinate and grow only if conditions are favourable: with enough moisture to rehydrate the food reserves and with warmth and air for the embryo to breathe, make new cell tissue and enlarge. During germination the embryo is totally dependent on the food reserves in the seed but once the seedling starts to grow green leaves it will need a regular supply of other nutrients.

As the seedling develops, the primary root forces its way down into the soil, and the primary stem starts to grow upwards towards the light. Once the leaves have expanded the seedling starts to manufacture life-sustaining starches and sugars – a process called *photosynthesis* for which light is essential; without it, the seedling stops growing, withers and eventually dies.

Basically, what happens in photosynthesis is this: when light reacts with the green pigment (*chlorophyll*) in the leaves, carbon dioxide from the air combines with water within the leaf, forming simple hydrocarbons like starch and sugar. Any surplus to immediate needs is turned into high-energy sugars, waxes and oils and stored for future use. During the process of photosynthesis, oxygen, a by-product, is given off from the leaves – one of the factors that makes trees important in oxygen-starved cities.

The sugars and other reserves are broken down to water in a further process known as *respiration* which is at its peak in actively growing trees in spring and summer.

The numerous pores (*stomata*) on the surface of the leaves regulate the exchange of gas and moisture between the tree and the atmosphere. The pores open when the leaves are fully charged with moisture. Only then can the processes of photosynthesis and respiration go ahead. During a prolonged drought, the pores shut and the process slows dramatically. Without moisture, the tree would eventually wither and die.

Slowly, as secondary roots and branches grow, the seedling tree becomes increasingly complex. With each succeeding year the trunk lengthens and widens in girth – as you can see if you look at the 'annual rings' in a sawn tree trunk.

The inner tissues of the stem or trunk form an elaborate plumbing system which conveys the mineral-rich moisture upwards from the roots of the tree to the topmost parts, and the starches and sugars downwards from its leaves to its other parts. Surrounding the inner tissues is an outer layer, called the *cambium*, protected in turn by the bark. If a tree is injured it is the cambium that forms a new protective layer. When propagating, it is through the cambium that buds and grafts are united to their rootstocks.

The tree's roots have a dual role – to provide support and anchorage for the tree and to tap into the reserves of nutrients and moisture in the soil. As the tree grows, it establishes both thick, sinker roots for anchorage and for combating drought, and finer, shallower, fibrous roots which draw moisture and nutrients from the surface of the soil. Healthy trees need a balance between sinker and fine roots, which can be disturbed if older trees are transplanted: the fibrous roots grow at the expense of the sinkers.

Although the branch arrangement of any tree is influenced by its genetic make-up – as indeed are its other qualities – the shape and form can be altered by pruning, training and the way it is cultivated. Differences in soil, site and climate can also affect the appearance of a tree.

Leaf fall and autumn colour, for example, in deciduous trees are a direct result of a seasonal drop in temperature. The cells at the base of each leaf thicken and this shuts off the water and nutrient supply to the leaf blades. Simultaneously chlorophyll is broken down, resulting in pigmentation changes – to reds, browns, yellows and blues.

Self-seeding
The survival of trees in the wild depends to some extent on how efficiently the various species can despatch their seeds away from the canopy of the tree, ensuring that they have sufficient light and nutrients to grow into seedlings. The five illustrations on these pages show some of the different methods:

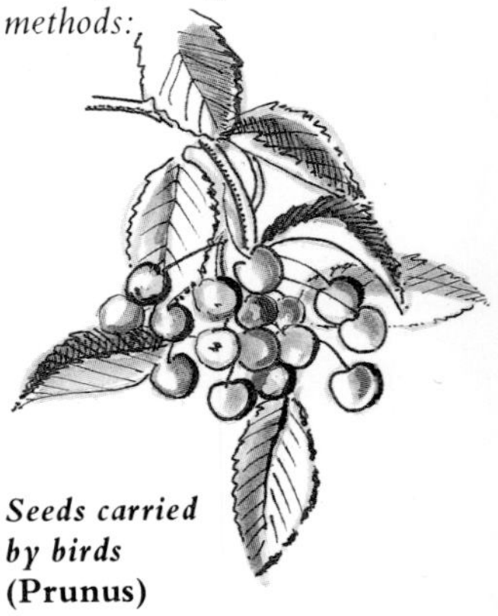

Seeds carried by birds **(Prunus)**

Seeds carried by wind **(Acer)**

Cross-section of tree trunk
In the plumbing system of the tree the sapwood stores the nutrients and carries them from one part of the tree to another. The phloem takes starches and sugars down from the leaves. The cambium forms new tissue while the bark acts as a skin, protecting the inner tissues. The heartwood in the centre of the tree stores waste matter.

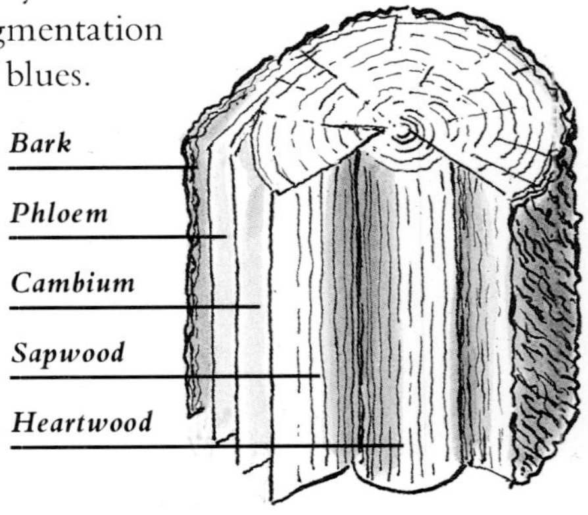

Flowers are a sign of maturity. Once flowering and fruiting begin the growth of the tree slows down. But before seed and fruit can be produced, the flowers have to be pollinated and fertilized. Pollination is the transfer of pollen, by wind or insects, from the *stamens* (male) to the *stigma* (female) of the flower. With some trees, including many hollies, the pollen must be transferred from a male flowering tree on to a female flowering variety – hence the need to grow male and female varieties close together.

Given suitable levels of warmth, moisture and nutrition – mainly from the plant's reserves – fertilization and fruit/seed setting follow naturally after flowering and successful pollination.

Eventually, weakened by old age, pests and diseases, the tree comes to the end of its useful life and dies. In the case of some trees, that can be several hundred years.

Classifying trees

The difference between trees and shrubs was analysed in the Introduction. Botanists have classified trees, as indeed they have all other plants, not just as an academic exercise but to help with identification and selection as well as with care and cultivation. Seed plants are divided into two major classes, angiosperms and gymnosperms. Within these are further subdivisions, including families. The families, in turn, are divided into groups, each of which is called a *genus* (pl = *genera*). Some families contain several genera with broadly similar botanical characteristics: for example, *Rosaceae* (the rose family) includes the following genera: flowering quince (*Chaenomeles*); *Cotoneaster*; thorn (*Crataegus*); apple (*Malus*); pear (*Pyrus*); and peach, plum and cherry (all *Prunus*). All of these have flowers with five (or multiples of five) petals and all produce stones or pip-like seeds enclosed in pulpy fruits.

Each genus can be sub-divided again into *species* (although a few contain one species only). Trees within a species usually differ little from each other, and if you cannot obtain your first choice, a close relative will often make a good substitute. Similarly, if a tree planted for fruit, nuts or berries has a close relative near by, it may solve any problems with poor pollination.

Trees are normally referred to by their genus and species names, written in Latin in italics. The genus comes first with a capital letter, for example, *Magnolia* and the specific epithet after it, with a small initial letter, for example, *Magnolia stellata*. You will sometimes see a further name, in Latin or in English, after the species name. This denotes some variant in the species. Although not strictly correct botanically, nurserymen usually refer to all these additional names as 'varietal'. Naturally occurring varieties are catalogued with a small letter, i.e. *Magnolia kobus var. stellata*. The varietal name here, and in most other cases, is descriptive – *stellata* means 'star-like'. Nursery-bred varieties (*cultivars*) – often the result of crossing dissimilar parents of the same species – are catalogued with a capital letter and enclosed in inverted commas, i.e. *Magnolia kobus var. stellata* 'Water Lily'.

Beware of trees with seemingly similar names – they can look very different from each other at maturity. For instance, *Tsuga canadensis* makes a large forest tree but a specially cultivated form, *Tsuga canadensis* 'Jeddeloh', is only a 30-cm (12-in) high midget.

Trees catalogued with an '×' between the genus and species names or an '×' before their name are usually the result of crosses between different species within the same genus. Those with an '×' before their name are the result of a cross between two different genera.

Although English common names are often easier to remember and sound less forbidding, they can often be an unreliable guide to a tree's true identity. For instance the true cedars hail from the genus *Cedrus* but Tasmanian Cedar = *Athrotaxis*, Incense Cedar = *Calocedrus decurrens*, Japanese Cedar = *Cryptomeria japonica* and Western Red Cedar = *Thuja plicata*. Although commonly called cedars, these trees have a leaf formation that is quite different from the true cedars.

In early times it was not unknown for several plant hunters to discover the same tree and give it different names. Nowadays, the internationally accepted procedure is to rename trees so that their first recorded name is used. For example the Incense Cedar, formerly *Libocedrus decurrens*, is today referred to as *Calocedrus decurrens*.

Seeds carried by animals, such as squirrels
(Quercus)

Seeds carried on water
(Salix)

Seeds with a trigger mechanism which expels the seed from the seed-pod
(Hamamelis)

ORIGINS & DISTRIBUTION

GARDEN TREES today are a very mixed lot, originating from many lands. On plant expeditions, seeds and living materials, collected mainly from the wild, were brought back to botanic gardens, generous sponsors and the leading nurseries of the day, which then introduced them to the general public.

Tree characteristics

A tree is influenced by both inherited qualities and acquired characteristics.

As previously mentioned, tree habit and the colour and form of leaf and flower are all passed down from previous generations. When growing trees from seed, the offspring will be identical to the parent only if the seed was either the result of crossing trees of the same species, or from the self-fertilization of flowers of a true species (even these plants can vary slightly). But if trees are propagated by cuttings, budding or grafting (in which the tree is grown on the roots of another) you can confidently expect parents and offspring to look alike.

Acquired features are of less significance than inherited ones since they are largely the result of know-how, pruning, training and fertilizing, over which there is a considerable degree of control. The prevailing site, soil and climate and the cultural treatment all influence the final outcome – particularly the size of the tree.

When choosing a tree, it is worth studying its natural habitat. Details of the original site, soil and climate provide the key to the suitability or otherwise of the tree for a particular region.

The most critical factors affecting growth are the temperature (see hardiness, below) and moisture. Trees like swamp cypresses (*Taxodium*), which originate in moist sites and areas of high rainfall, are not adapted to survive extremely arid conditions. Many trees also show a marked preference when it comes to soil: for light or heavy, acid or alkaline types.

Hardiness is of major importance when choosing trees. You must ensure they are hardy enough to thrive locally. Few difficulties are likely to arise if native trees are planted, but as many attractive garden trees originate from foreign parts, you must check first.

Selecting trees

Never buy a tree on impulse just because it looks good at the time – remember, it is likely to be a major feature in the garden for many years to come. Ask yourself what purpose the tree serves: if the tree is purely for aesthetic effect, for example? Or is it to provide screening, privacy and seclusion? Or are edible crops the aim?

Another good idea is to make a list of trees that appeal, eliminate those unlikely to tolerate the prevailing growing conditions (check the hardiness, for example), and then choose from what is left, bearing in mind the following points.

The ultimate space needed must be calculated (see pages 100-163 where height of individual trees is given), not forgetting to take into account the proximity of the tree to buildings, drains and other services. In heavy soils, no tree should be planted closer to a building than a distance equal to its ultimate height. If the soil is sandy and well-drained, this does not apply except with poplars and willows which have invasive roots capable of damaging drains and building foundations. For these the rule is that they should not be planted nearer than twice the distance of their eventual height. Check the information about any tree to make sure that it is suited to the soil in your garden. (Soil preparation is discussed on page 170.) A simple pH kit can be used to assess the acidity or alkalinity of the soil.

Trees that have bad habits or create work are best avoided. Large-leaved trees like horse chestnuts and some maples can be a nuisance at leaf-fall if planted near paths, drains and gutters. The excessive suckering of some species of *Prunus* will make it difficult to mow a lawn near by; various *Crataegus* and *Malus* need a lot of pruning to keep them in shape. Remember that falling fruits and bird droppings are a problem when fruit trees are planted near paths and seating areas.

What size to buy?

For instant effect or early cropping, the older the tree – within limits – the quicker the result, though some trees, like *Magnolia*, thrive best if planted when small. However, the cost of older trees can be prohibitive and getting them established can be tricky. With some trees – particu-

Checklist

Check the name and hardiness.

Opt for trees with a well-balanced framework of branches. The main stem should be straight and strong and of a thickness in proportion to the height. The biggest in the batch is not necessarily the best.

Look for healthy foliage with good colour. Avoid bare-stemmed trees, especially conifers.

With fruiting trees consider pollinator varieties. Family trees, where two or more varieties have been grafted onto one tree, are excellent where space is at a premium.

With grafted trees avoid any showing a lot of suckering (unwanted shoots near soil level which weaken the tree). Avoid trees with large unsightly graft unions.

With container-grown trees, avoid any which are wilting or have dried out with shrinking compost; any which are badly pot-bound, are too big for their container or have rooted into the ground; any which show signs of movement – go for firmly anchored, well-rooted trees.

Balled-and-wrapped trees should have a firm, moist – not crumbly – rootball.

Avoid bare-root trees with dried or shrivelled roots. Look for plenty of vigorous, healthy roots to support the tree after planting.

Steer clear of pre-packed trees with white roots growing into the peat packing and those showing signs of premature opening of buds.

larly with conifers or any trees that are top-heavy compared with their root system – there is a risk that they will be unstable at maturity.

Evergreens In general these are bought at a smaller size and younger age than their deciduous counterparts. They are categorized as follows:

Seedlings and transplants, sold for 'growing on' (ie for you to cultivate until they are mature enough to be planted out) and for bonsai, will vary from a few inches to 30 cm (12 in) or more in height.

Liners and whips – young trees of about 20-60 cm (8-24 in) in height – can be planted out in their final positions but will do better if grown on for a year or two.

Standard nursery stock varies enormously in shape and comes ready for planting out in its final position – in sizes from 20 cm (8 in) for dwarf conifers up to 1.5 m (5 ft) for tall evergreens.

Deciduous trees These are categorized as:

Seedlings and transplants (young plants) sold for growing on – 30-90 cm (12-36 in) in height. The smallest are suitable for bonsai.

Liners and whips are sold to grow and train as required. Single-stemmed, they vary from 1-1.5 m (3-5 ft) in height.

Standard nursery stock can be planted in their final positions – 1.5-3 m (5-10 ft) in height.

Advanced nursery stock (extra heavy) are trees of between 3.5-6 m (12-20 ft) in height; they are more expensive and need careful handling.

Semi-mature trees, the largest category – up to 9 m (30 ft) high – although available, are very expensive.

Edible and ornamental trees of planting size can usually be bought either as free-standing specimens or as ready-trained espalier forms.

Free-standing forms

Bushes make compact trees for small gardens where underplanting is not envisaged. Recommended for fruit. A short 30-60-cm (12-24-in) trunk is topped with a forked crown of branches.

Standards – the normal full standard tree has 1.5-1.8 m (5-6 ft) of clear stem beneath a forked framework of branches. They give height and shade and allow underplanting.

Half-standards with shorter trunks make smaller trees. Weeping trees are also sold as standards or half-standards. Excellent for ornamental use.

Feathered or pyramid is the term used to describe a tree with a vertical central leader carrying a succession of branches starting near ground level. They are used both for fruit crops and as ornamental trees.

Ready-trained trees

These utilize vertical space against a wall or fence and are ideal for fruit crops in small gardens.

Cordon – typically has a single stem set at an oblique angle. Twin vertical-stemmed forms are sometimes available. Apples and pears make good cordon crops.

Fan – a semi-circle of branches radiates out from a short trunk. Popular for edible peaches and pears, but the Flowering Almond (*Prunus dulcis*) also does well in this form.

Espalier – has a tiered arrangement of pairs of horizontal branches. Edible crops respond well to this treatment and so do some ornamental trees, e.g. *Ginkgo* and *Laburnum*.

Rootstocks and roots

Since a tree is only as good as its roots, the rootstock should be considered as well. Trees can be prepared for sale in various ways:

A container-grown tree comes in the pot in which it was grown with its roots undisturbed. When well grown, it is worth the extra cost every time. Plant at any time except during frost or drought or when the ground is waterlogged.

Balled-and-wrapped trees are field-grown. Dug up with a good ball of soil, packed around with moist peat and wrapped in plastic, net or burlap, they make a good second best to container trees. Plant in autumn or spring.

Bare-root trees are also field-grown but when lifted most of the soil is shaken off. They are difficult to re-establish, but those packed in moist peat are likely to suffer the least setback. Only suitable for autumn and early spring planting.

Pre-packed trees are virtually bare-root, usually marketed in protective plastic packs. Suitable for early spring planting.

Many trees don't take very kindly to bare-root or pre-packing treatment. It is always best to buy broadleaved evergreens and conifers container grown or balled and wrapped.

Suppliers and sources
There are several different sources of supply and each has particular advantages and disadvantages.

GARDEN CENTRES are popular. You can usually have a good look round at most times of the year to see what is on offer. Many centres have trained staff on hand to answer questions but the range is often limited.

SHOPS AND STORES are often cheap, but carry stocks for a very limited season with no qualified advice on hand. Frequently trees are kept at high temperatures for several weeks, which weakens them. When planted out they may never fully recover.

MAIL ORDER is convenient and prices are usually competitive, but be sure to take possible high transit and packaging costs into account. Also, trees are bought unseen and may have to travel long distances in cramped packaging.

SPECIALIST NURSERIES are best for unusual varieties. Expert advice, based on a wide experience of their stock, is usually available but prices can be high.

PREPARATION FOR PLANTING

ONCE YOU HAVE decided on the layout details and planting positions of your trees you can push ahead with all the preparatory work, such as checking that trees will be delivered on time, making sure tools and equipment, particularly if you are hiring them, will be to hand when needed and organizing stakes, ties, manures, fertilizers, mulches, containers, composts and planting mixtures. If contractors are to be called in, you should obtain several quotations and engage firms in good time.

On a new site, clear away any debris and builders' rubble. Prune back overcrowded trees and shrubs to let in light and air for new trees. (As a guide, deal with evergreens in summer and deciduous trees in winter.)

If any levelling of the ground is needed it should be tackled next, but take care not to bury good topsoil under infertile subsoil. Wherever possible adopt the 'cut and fill' principle of using surplus soil from high spots to fill in low areas. And do make the effort to fork up compacted ground – particularly any legacies from construction work.

Drainage

It is important that you do any drain-laying before planting your trees if they are not to suffer. Poor drainage is best approached from several angles.

First deal with the subsoil. In the average garden, agricultural land drains are often impractical. The solution can lie in the construction of rubble-filled soakaways (right).

Next aim to divert water running off adjacent higher land and hard-surfaced areas by digging out a system of trenches, positioned to trap the water. Make them 30 cm (12 in) deep and wide, fill them with rubble topped off with gravel and run them to a soakaway set at a lower level.

Finally, improve the flow of water through the soil by good cultivation (see soil preparation, right).

In areas of heavy rainfall, growing trees in raised beds or containers may provide the best answer to poor natural drainage, as it does when ground conditions are otherwise unsatisfactory. For example, when:

☐ The soil is shallow and poor or a thin layer of good topsoil overlies impenetrable rock.

☐ Existing soils are infertile due to excess alkalinity, salinity or pollution.

☐ The subsoil in your garden is chalk and a lime-hater is the chosen tree.

☐ Trees are to be grown in hard-surfaced areas where there are no pockets of soil.

Soil preparation

Extra care is called for when trees are planted on land recently cleared of other trees. There is a risk of carry-over of pests and diseases – especially if the original tree died.

Soil disinfection is vital if you are replanting on the exact spot from which a diseased tree has been removed. Take away obviously infected soil before forking up around the hole and drenching with a proprietary soil disinfectant – cresylic acid and other tar oil derivatives are excellent. Most are applied when the soil is warm, and are best covered for 48 hours or so afterwards to keep in the fumes. Follow the makers' instructions (dilutions and application rates vary), use protective clothing if specified and take care not to harm nearby plants. Delay planting until all fumes have dispersed and test the soil by sowing mustard and cress. Deal with infected tools at the same time.

In towns and cities, the long-term accumulation of soot and grime can make soils acid and infertile. Liming, manuring and the discriminate use of fertilizer can all help.

Although many trees will grow on both acid and alkaline soils, some have strong preferences.

The acid/alkaline status of soil is normally expressed in terms of pH. In practice the range varies from about pH4 = acid to about pH8.5 = alkaline. A pH of 6.5 to 7 is about neutral with sufficient lime for most trees. Some trees like *Arbutus* and *Liquidambar* become unhealthy with yellowing chloritic leaves if the pH rises above 6.5. Others like *Prunus* do not thrive when the pH is 5 or less.

Soil pH is important with trees as with shrubs and should not be ignored. It is worth establishing the pH level – especially if it is in question – with a simple DIY soil test before buying trees. The instructions are easy to follow and results are read off on a pH scale using a colour comparison chart. A direct-dial electric pH meter is another alterna-

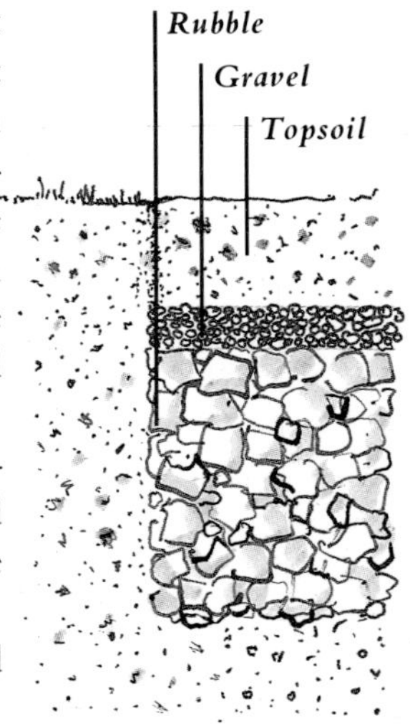

Soakaway
At the lowest point of the problem area, excavate a hole 75 cm (2½ ft) square and 1 m (3 ft) deep. Fill it to within 30 cm (12 in) of the top with clean rubble, levelling and consolidating after each 15-cm (6-in) layer is added. Failure to firm risks subsidence later on. Spread a 5-cm (2-in) layer of gravel before finally levelling off with topsoil – which should have been kept to one side when digging out the hole. Expect one such soakaway to drain an area of 20 sq m (25 sq yd).

tive. However, only the more expensive models are entirely reliable. Some garden centres and horticultural companies provide soil-testing services at little cost.

You can correct minor soil acidity by applying ground limestone at the rate indicated by a soil test, but correcting very alkaline soil is fraught with difficulties. If you have very alkaline soil, either choose alkaline-tolerant species or grow any lime-haters in raised beds or containers.

Preparation of beds and borders

Dwarf and slow-growing garden trees, along with nursery stock being grown on for transplanting, are often grown in beds and borders. The better you prepare the ground for the trees, the more quickly they will establish themselves.

Double digging is recommended. In the process, pick out difficult perennial weeds and large stones and fork in generous quantities of well-rotted garden compost, manure or peat. If the land is very weedy, clean it up during the growing season when persistent hoeing, forking or rotavating will weaken and kill most weeds. Also, weedkillers are usually most effective if applied during spring and early summer when weeds are actively growing. Be sure to follow makers' instructions and to leave the recommended time between application and planting.

Just before planting, top-dress the soil with 3 cm (1 in) of peat, processed bark or similar – plus general fertilizer and bonemeal – forking it all lightly into the top 10 cm (4 in) of soil and then raking the surface level. In average situations a fertilizer supplying 7 per cent each of nitrogen, phosphate and potassium, applied at the rate of 70 g per sq m (2 oz per sq yd) is about right. Apply bonemeal at a similar rate.

Where the soil is very dry, gently apply 10 litres of water per sq m (2 gallons per sq yd) some 24 hours before planting. This will moisten about 10 cm (4 in) in depth. Where the soil is dry to a greater depth, increase pro rata.

Preparation of planting pockets

It is usual to plant larger free-standing trees, all wall-trained varieties and single specimens in grass or hard-surfaced areas into planting pockets.

For standard nursery stock (see page 169), dig out pockets at least 60 cm (2 ft) in diameter and 45-60 cm ($1\frac{1}{2}$-2 ft) deep. In all cases, there should be 15 cm (6 in) between the roots and the sides of the hole. If the evacuated soil is poor, take it away, and loosen up the sides and bottom of the hole, before forking in a bucketful of well-rotted manure, garden compost or moistened peat, plus a cupful of bonemeal. On heavy soil, work in a bucketful of organic matter and sand at the same time to aerate the soil.

Always be mindful that, as a general rule, no free-standing tree should be planted closer to a building than a distance equal to its ultimate spread. Nor should any wall-trained tree be planted closer to a wall than 30 cm (12 in) due to problems of dryness and instability.

If it is necessary to restrict tree roots to prevent damage to foundations, services or drains, or to promote fruiting (with trees like figs), grow the trees in containers or construct a 'tree box' as a good second best. (It is not particularly difficult to make one.) Excavate a hole 90 cm (3 ft) in diameter and of a similar depth at a point where there is no danger of interfering with underground services. Line it with 11 cm ($4\frac{1}{2}$ in) of concrete or a single brick wall. Bottom out with a 30-cm (12-in) layer of consolidated rubble before part-filling with planting mix.

To give the tree a good start it is worth either buying in or preparing your own backfill soil mixture with which to fill the planting hole. Standard potting composts are most popular and soil-based mixtures are normally best. However, soil-less kinds are favoured for lime-hating varieties. Trees settle down and become established more quickly if there is no sudden transition of rooting medium, from peat to soil and vice versa, for example.

Less well known are fertilized and fortified planting mixes based on organic peat or bark soil conditioners. Although they are gaining in popularity they need careful handling.

Home-made mixes involve work but usually work out cheaper than the bought-in product. They come into their own where existing topsoil is reasonable – weed-, pest- and disease-free – and really needs only fertifying.

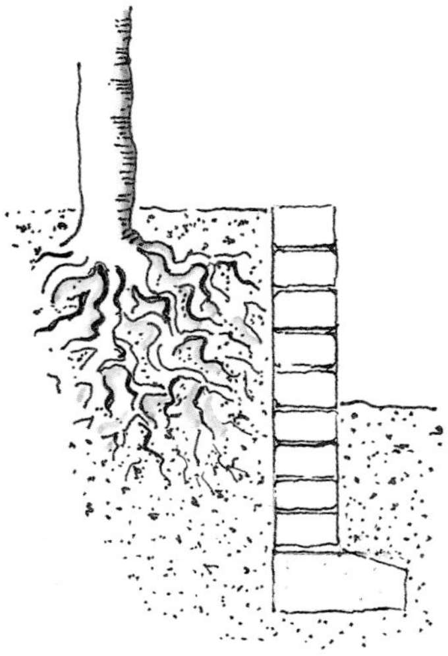

Making a raised bed
A useful bed size for a single tree is a minimum of 60 × 60 cm (2 × 2 ft), increasing to 1.2 × 1 m (4 × 3 ft) for a small group. Brick, stone and concrete are the most durable materials – minimum thickness 11 cm ($4\frac{1}{2}$ in). Build on a 10 cm (4 in) thick and 20 cm (8 in) wide concrete foundation with provision for drainage in the bottom side walls. The average garden tree, ultimately growing to say 6 m (20 ft), needs a minimum 60-cm (2-ft) depth of good topsoil. To minimize drying out and the need for summer watering, no more than two-thirds of the bed should be above ground.

Planting

*H*AVING ORGANIZED all the preparatory work, water all container-grown trees an hour or two before planting and allow to drain before disturbing. Plunge small containers and small balled-and-wrapped trees – complete with wrapping – into a bucket of water, barely covering the rootball. Remove and drain as soon as the air bubbles stop rising – usually about 20 minutes. Plunge bare-root trees into a tank of clean water, leave overnight and then plant the next morning, ensuring that the roots are kept covered until planting.

Supporting trees

Any tree you plant will need some support to ensure that the roots stay firmly anchored in the soil after planting. Contrary to popular belief you are stabilizing the foundations of the tree, rather than simply supporting the stem, when you stake a tree. Modern practice encourages the use of shorter stakes – a third of the height of the tree.

A free-standing tree (unless very young) is traditionally tied to a timber stake. Avoid badly knotted timber – it is apt to snap in high winds – and treat all stakes with a safe horticultural preservative before use.

When calculating the length of stake required, for stakes up to 2.4 m (8 ft) allow for 45-60 cm (18-24 in) to be sunk into the ground. For stakes longer than this, 25 per cent of their total length needs to be below ground. When staking bush trees, the stake should be up to the lowest branch. With standards and half-standards – 5 cm (2 in) below. Any surplus should be sawn off before fixing the ties. Always relate the thickness of the stake to the length. Metal stakes are more durable than timber but there is a greater risk of chafing.

After planting (see page 174) the stem of the tree is tied to the stake. Proprietary adjustable ties are the best bet – even if they are more expensive than home-made. Whatever the type, make sure it has a spacer to keep the trunk and the stake apart. At the cheaper end of the range are simple plastic strips, which are looped around the trunk with both ends nailed to the stake, but these are a nuisance to adjust.

Never be tempted to tie trees with wire – it cuts into the bark and can kill the tree. If you use string or cord you must protect the bark by inserting at least two or three layers of hessian between the trunk and the tie.

The following are the most commonly used methods of staking:

Cane support The traditional method of tying a very young tree to a bamboo cane has altered little, although bamboo canes are giving way to stronger, cleaner and longer-lasting thin, tubular metal stakes and plastic ties are taking over from tarred twine. If not transferred along with the tree, the support is put in place at planting time, a quarter of its height into the soil. Ensure ties are no more than 20-30 cm (8-12 in) apart.

Single vertical stake – the most widely used method of staking garden trees (below). Secure a bush tree to its stake with one tie immediately below the bottom branch. Standards and half-standards are normally fastened with two: one at the top of the stake and the other half-way down.

Oblique stakes are useful when it is impractical to drive stakes in vertically near the tree trunk (below). They can be hammered home after planting without risk of injury to roots. They also give a greater degree of support in windy gardens.

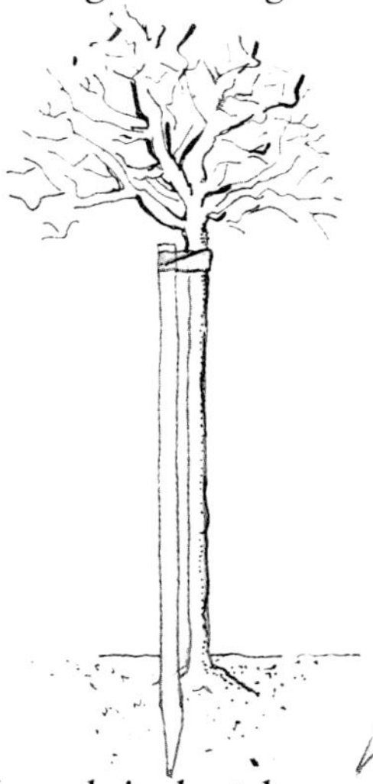

Normal single stake
Set the stake vertically in the planting hole and drive it home slightly off-centre and ideally into the direction of the prevailing wind. This is so that the tree is blown away from the stake rather than towards it, reducing the risk of chafing.

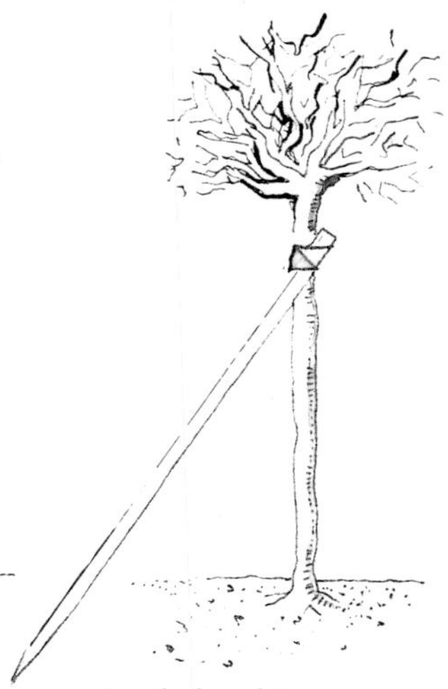

Angled staking
Drive in a single stake at a 45° angle some distance out from the tree. Aim to point the top into the prevailing wind and position it slightly below the lowest branch. Secure the tree to the stake with a single tie where the two meet.

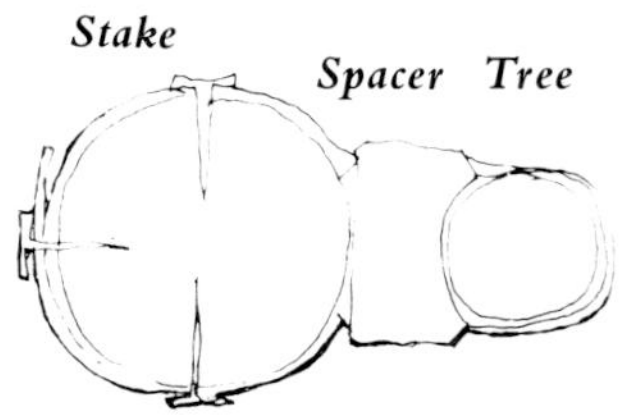

Proprietary tree-tie with built-in spacer to prevent chafe

Double and triple vertical stakes are usually reserved for heavier trees. With the double stake method, stakes are driven into the ground one on each side of the trunk. A long tree tie is looped round the trunk and both ends fixed to one of the stakes. A second tie is then looped around and fixed to the other stake so that the ties pull against each other. The triple stake is similar. Three stakes are evenly spaced round the tree and the trunk supported by a three-way pull.

Twin stakes with cross bar give a more rigid anchorage than double stakes. Bolt on one or more crossbars and tie the trunk to these.

Maypole supports are used almost exclusively for heavy cropping fruits – ideal for apples grown as dwarf bushes. Drive a minimum 3-m (10-ft) stake into the planting hole and then support each of the main branches by wires wound maypole fashion. One end of each wire is attached to the top of the stake and the other to a 'mini-cradle' of plastic supporting the branch about half-way between trunk and branch extremity. The wire must not come into direct contact with the branch as it will cut into it.

Guying is used at planting time to support semi-mature trees with a strong central trunk. It is also a useful way to stabilize old trees. For reasons of shape or size, newly moved semi-mature trees can be difficult to support. Those with a large, firm rootball may be anchored by means of 'deadmen' timbers and root guying – techniques best left to experienced tree surgeons.

Wall-trained trees Wires and wall fixings form the basis of most wall supports for both ornamentals and fruit trees in gardens. One popular and well-tried method is to use 12-14 gauge, taut, horizontal wires fixed to the wall with vine eyes. The threaded type, which are screwed into previously drilled and plugged holes, are preferable to the hammer-in type. Set the vine eyes no more than 1.2 m (4 ft) apart. Secure the bottom wire about 50 cm (20 in) above the ground with successive wires a similar distance apart one above the other. With cordon- and fan-trained trees attach bamboo canes to the wires and tie in the branches to these at 15-30-cm (6-12-in) intervals. With espaliers, adjust the spacings to suit branch arrangement.

Fence-trained trees Attach a series of horizontal wires to the fence posts, provided they are no wider apart than the usual 1.8 m (6 ft).

How you plant the trees depends on their stage of development at the time you plant, and how they have been supplied.

Young nursery trees

Container growing is the norm (see page 180). However, in a reasonably sheltered garden, planting in a nursery bed is fine – set so that the top of the rootball is about 1 cm (½ in) below the surrounding soil level. Water to settle the soil and mulch with pulverized bark or compost.

Bare-root trees

Bare-root planting is recommended only for deciduous trees and for nothing larger than standard nursery stock. Even here there are exceptions – *Laburnum, Robinia* and *Cercis* should be set out as container-grown stock.

Plant during late winter or early spring while the trees are still dormant. Trees then have a chance to put out new roots before they have to cope with the strain of leafing up and with drying spring winds. Keeping the roots covered with damp sacking, set the tree in position against the stake so that the soil mark on the stem is slightly below the surrounding ground. Add or remove backfill soil to adjust the tree level and check the level by laying a cane horizontally across the top of the hole. Loosely tie the tree to the stake or get someone to hold it steady while work proceeds. Spread out the roots, trimming back any which are damaged to sound wood and barely covering them with planting mix. Joggle the stem slightly to work the mix down between the roots. Add more planting mix and firm it in by treading and heeling, levelling it off with the surrounding soil. It is best to fix ties immediately after planting – not before – to allow for any settlement during planting.

Balled-and-wrapped and container trees

Balled-and-wrapped evergreen trees are best set out during autumn or spring. Deciduous kinds can be planted out during mild spells in winter as ground conditions allow. Container-grown trees

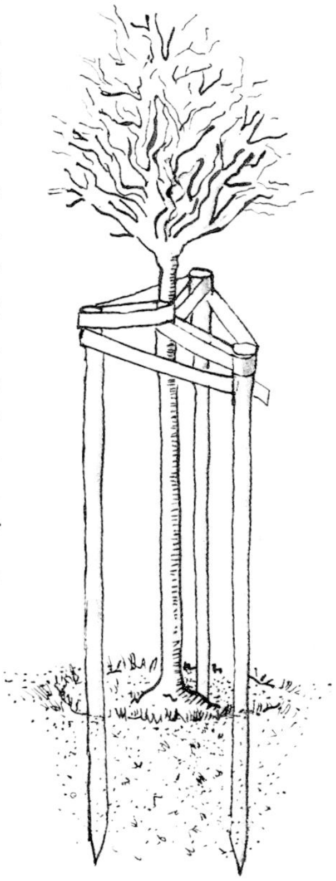

Triple stake
Space the three stakes evenly around the tree in triangular formation. Loop each tie round the trunk and then around each stake, as shown.

Planting a tree

1 Prepare the soil (see page 170) and dig out a pocket large enough to leave 15 cm (6 in) space between the rootball and the sides of the planting hole. Add manure and a cupful of bonemeal.

2 Tap the container to loosen the rootball, remove the tree from its container and gently tease out the roots, trimming any if necessary.

3 Insert the tree in the prepared planting hole, and check that the base of the stem is level with the top of the planting hole.

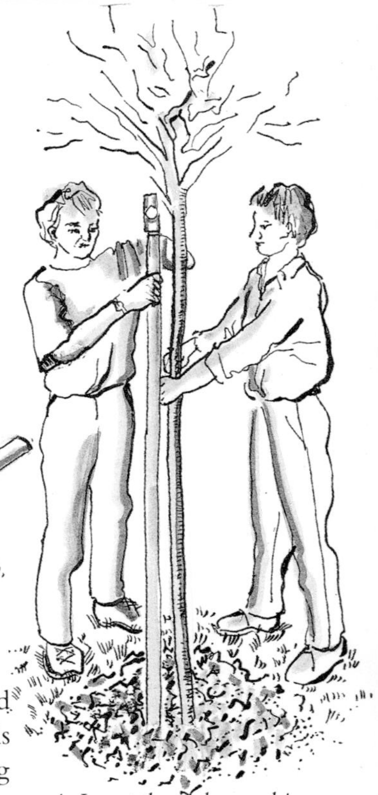

4 Insert the stake, making a V-shaped space in between the roots to prevent damage to the rootball, and backfill the hole with topsoil.

5 Firm down the soil and fasten the stake to the tree with an appropriate tie (see page 172). Water the area round the tree thoroughly and then cover with a mulch.

can be set out at almost any time of year except high summer, provided the soil is not frozen, saturated or bone-dry. But even with container-grown trees, spring or autumn planting is preferable and should always be the first choice for evergreen trees.

Planting balled-and-wrapped trees

Move them carefully to their planting positions. Those which are too big to manhandle in comfort can be eased onto a plastic sheet and dragged into place. If need be, break down one side of the planting hole to form a ramp down which to slide the rootball. Re-adjust the level of the rootball so that it is no more than about 3 cm (1 in) deeper than before the move. And as with any tree, ensure it is positioned so that its best side is shown to maximum effect. Loosely tie the tree to the support. Remove wrappings carefully so as not to disturb and break up the rootball. (This presents no problem with small trees, but with large ones leave a small piece of wrapping under the tree.)

Container-grown trees

A large container, complete with tree, is best eased into the planting hole before being cut away from the rootball. It is normal to remove a smaller container-grown tree from its container and then position it in its planting hole. Cut floppy containers open and peel them back, taking care not to damage young roots. Knock plants out of rigid pots; this should not be difficult if the compost is moist. Then gently tease out the roots encircling the rootball, without breaking up the ball of soil – roots left tangled at planting rarely grow freely into surrounding soil. As with bare-root trees, trim any roots that are damaged and loosely tie the tree to the stake to steady it. Work the planting mix around the rootball, firming it by heeling in after each 10-cm (4-in) layer is added and resisting the temptation to joggle the plant. Level off the soil and tie the tree to the stake.

Lifting, moving and planting semi-mature trees is carried out in autumn and spring and is usually best left to the professionals. Provision for deep watering should be made, regardless of soil and situation. Use four or more slightly angled drainpipes homed in on the rootball.

Large replanted rootballs are particularly prone to drying out. And it is not always easy to get water deep enough down. So when planting large balled and container-grown trees – especially in very dry situations – it is worth installing some form of deep-watering system (see page 176).

After planting

☐ Carry out any initial pruning (see page 178).
☐ Protect the roots of newly set out, autumn-planted frost-sensitive trees like *Magnolia* and some varieties of *Eucalyptus*. A 15-cm (6-in)

layer of straw, held in place with pegged down netting, works well.

☐ Protect all autumn-planted trees from cold and drying winds, particularly any evergreens. Shelter the trees on three sides with fine-mesh netting supported on canes or a light framework. Give rows and groups of trees shelter from prevailing winds by erecting a screen across the path of the prevailing wind. Fine-mesh netting or permeable fencing panels of, say, wattle, are both excellent forms of windbreak.

☐ Net wall-trained trees to protect them from bud stripping by birds.

☐ Where rabbits are likely to be troublesome, use proprietary metal or plastic tree guards.

☐ As soon as soil conditions allow, refirm trees lifted by frost or wind. And cover over any exposed roots with soil.

☐ During spring and summer, keep all newly planted trees well watered. Think in terms of about 2.5 cm (1 in) of water over the root zone each week.

☐ Give a heavy watering rather than a trickle, which will only encourage shallow rooting. Also hose down foliage, of evergreens in particular, after hot or dry windy days. In areas of low rainfall, it is a good idea to make a dish-shaped depression in spring around newly planted trees to stop any surface water running off. Scoop up loose surface soil to form a ridge some 60-90 cm (24-36 in) out from the trunk. In areas of heavy rainfall or in heavy soil, set the tree on a mound of soil, but ensure that the roots are covered.

☐ Also in spring, lightly hoe over the root run to break the soil crust. Remove any weeds, water well and apply a surface mulch of well-rotted garden compost, manure, peat or bark. Where supplies of suitable mulch are limited or expensive, consider black plastic perforated sheet, camouflaged under a very thin layer of gravel.

☐ Keep an eye on all stakes and ties, and adjust the ties as necessary.

Moving trees

If trees need re-siting in the garden, it is feasible to lift them and transplant them. Deciduous trees usually tolerate a move better than broadleaved evergreens and conifers. The larger the tree, the longer the preparation period needed and the greater the risk of damage.

Preparatory root pruning is best carried out in autumn. And when dealing with all but the smallest tree, which has not been in its present position more than five years, do it in two stages, starting two years before lifting.

The usual practice is to dig a semi-circular trench 30 cm (12 in) deep and of a similar width some 45-75 cm (18-30 in) out from the tree. However, for less damage to roots, take out two quarter-arc trenches on opposite sides of the tree. Either way, aim to make the diameter of the root-ball 12 times that of the trunk. Thick roots crossing the trench are severed, but fibrous ones are left unharmed. Backfill the trench with topsoil enriched with organic matter or use planting mix. Firm and heel as filling proceeds. Keep the tree watered and weed-free throughout the following season. In autumn, complete a circular trench round the tree. A year later the tree is ready for lifting.

Root pruning creates a compact ball of fibrous feeding roots, better able to sustain the tree when moved. It also controls vigour and can promote fruiting. After root pruning, thin the crown to ease the strain.

When lifting trees in readiness for replanting, ensure the soil is moist by watering it 24 hours beforehand or as necessary. Dig the soil away from round the tree – making the rootball 12 times the diameter of the trunk – and work under the rootball before rolling it on to a plastic sheet. Once the corners of the sheet are brought up round the trunk and tied, the tree is ready to move. A root-ball over 30 cm (12 in) in diameter is heavy and probably a two-person task.

Before moving bushy trees, always tie in the branches to make them manageable and to minimize the risk of breakage. Loop string around the middle of the tree and gently pull it fairly tight, then tie it. Large trees may need several ties.

Thin-barked trees like birch and lime may benefit from having their trunks wrapped before they are moved, as may large trees where the trunks are over 15 cm (6 in) in diameter. Simply wind strips of hessian or jute round the trunk for the first season or so for extra protection against any extremes of temperatures.

Root pruning
To prepare trees for transplanting or to control vigour, root pruning can be carried out. In the first year, dig out a trench about 75 cm (30 in) away from the trunk around the tree and about 30 cm (12 in) deep. Fill it with topsoil and organic matter. Keep the tree well watered and then the following year the tree can be lifted, with its now reduced rootball. If necessary, space the operation over a couple of years, digging out two quarter arcs the first year and completing the circle around the tree in the second year, which will give the tree longer to recover from the shock.

Feeding & Watering

Although ornamental trees in general need quite a bit of care and attention early in life, once they are established their demands are minimal until old age. Fruit trees and those grown in containers take up a great deal more time.

Watering

Watering, unless you live in an area with high rainfall, is important for the first year or two after planting, but from then on ornamental trees usually fend for themselves (container trees excepted, page 180). Heavy-cropping fruit trees – wall-trained peach, cherry and nectarine in particular – all benefit from some watering in dry summers.

Start watering as the soil begins to dry out in spring, and continue throughout summer. Be extra vigilant with newly planted container-grown and balled-and-wrapped trees. Very often the rootball is drier than the surrounding soil, which is deceptive until the new roots start to work. Consider using 'water signals' or a 'moisture meter' until experience is gained.

The amount of water to apply will vary according to local rainfall, the type of soil, the season and the weather. In hot, dry, drought-stricken conditions a minimum of 20 litres of water per sq m ($4\frac{1}{2}$ gallons per sq yd) per week is needed over the root-run (calculate the area out to the branch extremities). This equates with 3 cm (1 in) of rainfall. But you must be a bit flexible: be more generous for narrow columnar trees and assume a root-run of at least double the spread of the tree. Where provision has been made for deep watering (see below), water as normal down the drainpipes, then apply one third extra on the surface. Pay special attention to any tree that has been undercut prior to being moved as it must not dry out. With newly planted trees, it is better to soak the rootball rather than lightly water the whole area under the branches.

A watering can or a hose is the most effective and economical way to water trees in private gardens. Timing is essential with a hose, otherwise you may over or under water, with serious consequences. To work out the flow rate per minute, fill a bucket of known size with water, and calculate accordingly.

Fertilizers

To sustain growth trees need a balanced diet of nutrients. The 'macro-elements' – that is, nitrogen, phosphorus and potassium – are needed in the largest amounts. However, minute quantities of 'trace elements' like iron, magnesium, manganese, boron, zinc, copper and calcium are also essential for good health. In practice, deficiencies of macro-elements are the most common. But on occasions a shortage of iron, magnesium, manganese or calcium can cause problems. Deficiencies can normally be corrected by applying fertilizers or, for calcium, by liming.

Fertilizers supply concentrated nutrients and are variously described as quick-, average- or slow-acting. Since trees can only make use of nutrients that are in a weak, watery solution, the solubility governs the rate of uptake.

Be wary of manures sold under the guise of fertilizers. Most are more correctly soil condi-

Deep watering

Set two 30-cm (12-in) lengths of 8-cm (3-in) diameter drainpipe vertically, one on each side of the rootball with the top slightly exposed. Pack them around with planting mix and fill them with clean stones or gravel. Irrigation water poured in at the top will soak down to the roots. Water at regular intervals – up to two or three times a day in dry weather – when trying to get trees established. It will, if nothing else, aerate the rootball.

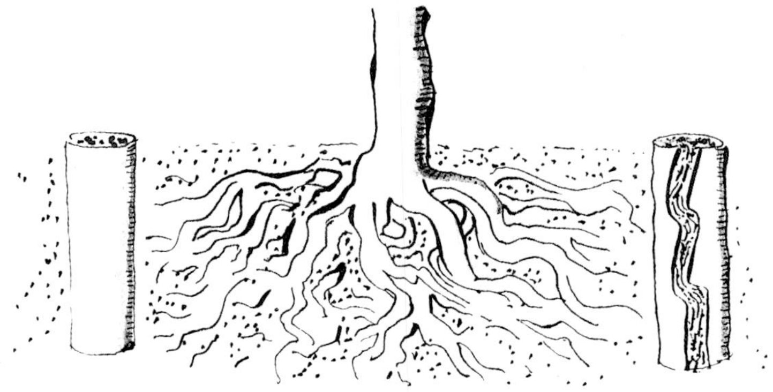

tioners intended for improving soil texture. And of those which justify the fertilizer tag, many are low in nutrients.

Use fertilizers strictly as directed – but less is safer than more – and always ensure the tree roots are moist before you apply them.

Pre-planting applications of average- to slow-acting fertilizers are normally applied dry and then worked into the bottom of the planting holes or raked into the topsoil of beds and borders: 50-70 g (2-3 oz) per standard nursery tree makes an average dressing. The traditional bonemeal has now been superseded by proprietary mixtures.

Post-planting top-dressing As a general rule don't feed newly planted trees for the first two years – unless planting in very poor soil. It is better to make the roots do their work. Later, give the trees a light dressing each spring, or in alternate years, scattered over the root-run prior to mulching. Hoe it into the top 3 cm (1 in) or so of soil. Surface-rooting trees such as many of the conifers, magnolias and strawberry trees (*Arbutus unedo*) are exceptions. And to avoid root damage simply spread on the dressing and water it in.

An average- to quick-acting general fertilizer should be applied at the rate of about 70 g per sq m (3 oz per sq yd). Where the trees are growing in grass, double the amount to compensate for competition from grass roots or, better still, for a metre around the tree prevent the grass from growing. Once fruit trees have started cropping, increase fertilizer rates. Mature trees can struggle on sandy or impoverished ground – so again application rates should be increased. Give heavier applications in two halves, 14 days apart. Another alternative is to boost dry fertilizers with liquid feeds during the summer months.

Subsoil feeding If trees have obviously been neglected and are not making reasonable growth, more drastic measures are required for the fertilizer, air and water to get down to the roots. Using a crowbar, make a series of holes in a broad band, starting about 60 cm (2 ft) out from the trunk and working systematically out to branch extremities. They should be about 5 cm (2 in) wide and 30 cm (12 in) deep and spaced about 60 cm (2 ft) apart. Autumn is a good time to tackle the job. Put down some slow-release fertilizer then fill the holes with full-strength soil-based potting compost, brush in, prod it home with a pointed stick, and water it to settle. Repeat the treatment every five years or so. Old trees growing in grass benefit from similar treatment.

Liquid feeding, applied as a soil drench, is mainly reserved for container-trees and for use where trees are obviously suffering or to give them a quick boost during the growing season.

If the garden overlies chalk or limestone, keep a close watch on any magnolias, *Arbutus* and parrotias. Should they fail to thrive and show signs of yellowing, give them a soil drench of iron sequestrene.

Foliar feeding of trees, by spraying very weak nutrient solutions onto the leaves, is again a useful way to correct nutrient deficiency and makes a good pick-me-up for recently planted trees.

Use only proprietary feeds intended for that purpose and do not apply sprays in higher concentrations than those recommended by the makers. Mix thoroughly and apply evenly in calm, overcast weather when the leaves are dry and the roots moist, to avoid leaf scorch

Mulching is an important, highly desirable, but often underrated job. It is especially beneficial for young trees – see page 175. It conserves soil moisture by reducing evaporation, keeps roots cool in hot sunshine and smothers weeds.

Mulch in spring once the soil has warmed up a bit. Where trees are growing in grass, maintain bare soil around the trunk to take the mulch.

In autumn when cleaning up round trees, lightly fork in mulch remains such as peat, manure or garden compost. Replenish bark and leave in place all year round. Top up the gravel over the plastic sheeting.

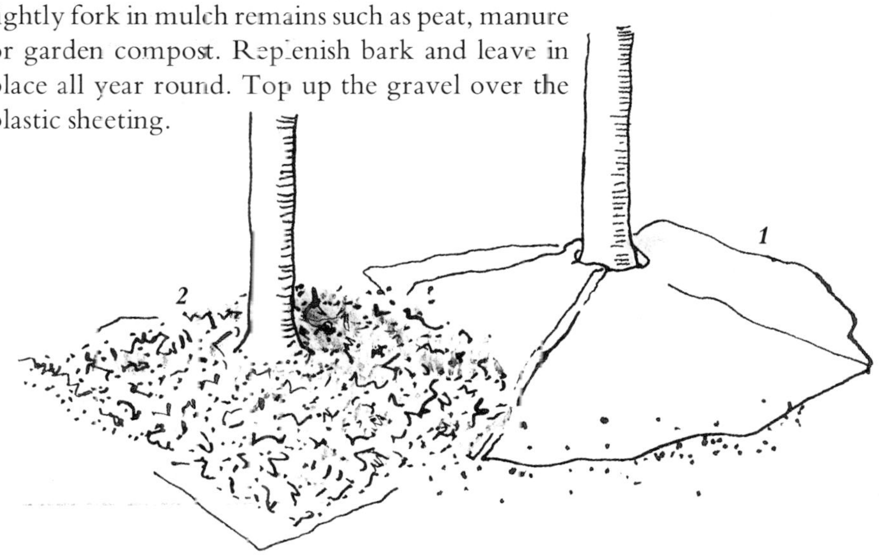

Mulching trees
*All young trees benefit if the area surrounding the trunk can be kept weedfree. Clean up around the tree, lightly fork in organic matter, and then cover with a sheet of black plastic, cut to fit neatly around the tree base (**1**). Cover the plastic with gravel to weight it down and to improve the appearance (**2**).*

Pruning

Sooner or later most trees grown in a garden situation will need some pruning. Whereas a forest tree usually prunes itself by losing some branches and growing fresh ones that shade out the older, lower ones (which die naturally or fall off, the small wounds healing over easily at the branch collar) trees grown as specimens produce larger low branches which often need to be removed. This should be done carefully because it will cause large wounds.

But tree pruning in the average garden is usually low key and rightly so, although it is a common failing to leave ornamental trees alone until they outgrow their space or start creating other problems. It is better to anticipate events and deal with the problem at an earlier stage. To summarize, pruning should be carried out:

☐ to maintain health and vigour and extend the life of the tree, as well as keeping it safe, by cutting dead and diseased wood back to sound tissue.

☐ to keep trees in shape and tidy by removing weak, spindly and inward pointing shoots and shortening back any crossing branches.

☐ to regulate and maintain flowering and fruit production.

In a small garden, where one or two trees are the norm, only brushwood and small branches will be dealt with. And so a good pair of pruners, a strong knife, a pair of loppers and a pruning saw should be enough – together with a notched pair of shears if small-leaved trees need to be clipped. Power saws, if needed, are best hired. All tools should be kept in good condition: clean, sharp, oiled and greased.

Pruning calendar

AUTUMN	*Deciduous free-standing and wall-trained trees. Free-standing evergreens in mild areas.*
WINTER	*As for autumn but exclude evergreens.*
SPRING	*Pollarding trees like willow and eucalyptus. Wall-trained stone fruits. Conifers and broad-leaved evergreens*
SUMMER	*Conifers and broad-leaved evergreens Wall-trained and intensive forms of fruits and ornamentals. Avoid heavy pruning in summer.*

When pruning young wood of up to pencil thickness, use a pruning knife or hand pruners and aim to cut cleanly to just above a plump, healthy bud. Slope the cut diagonally away from the bud to divert water and reduce the risk of rots. Thicker wood is best cut back to a vigorous branch or cut back to the swollen collar region. Avoid leaving short, blind stubs. They look untidy and they inevitably die back, becoming prone to disease. Smooth off any rough edges with a sharp knife. Do not paint the wounds – although often advised, it is of no help and can do positive harm.

If you need to increase headroom for planting and working, selectively remove some of the lower branches of the tree or trees, known as 'crown raising'. With trees like Silver Birch (*Betula pendula*), Paperbark Maple (*Acer griseum*) and Tibetan Cherry (*Prunus serrula*), crown raising can be used to expose the attractive bark to best advantage. In time evergreens – conifers in particular – tend to lose some of their lower branches. As they die they are best removed.

Where trees develop over-dense heads of foliage and branches – crab apple and thorn are notorious in this respect – cutting out light and air, 'crown thinning' is accepted practice, but the need for it can be over-emphasized.

The aim in crown thinning is to thin out the branches without reducing crown size. Cut out from the tree centre so that the remaining branches do not touch each other when in full leaf. Crown thinning is best restricted to deciduous trees and requires skill to achieve a balanced shape. With large trees, consult a tree surgeon.

Reducing both tree height and spread is called 'crown reduction'. Again it is best left to the experts on large trees. To reduce the height of single-main-stem trees it is normally safe to cut out the top just above a branch, reducing the height of the tree by no more than a third. Tall trees have to be cut back in sections – a dangerous job best left to specialists. Most deciduous varieties survive this treatment, as do evergreens, provided they are not too old. With multi-stem trees, shorten each branch by up to a third.

To reduce the overall spread of deciduous varieties the side branches are cut back, but evergreens should not be cut back into old wood.

General maintenance

Remove suckers (growths which arise at or near ground level) from the rootstocks of budded and grafted trees and from Robinia, *Lime and* Amelanchier *grown on their own roots.*

If single-stem trees start forking to produce two or more main stems, reduce these to the one best placed.

Shorten straggly, untidy or misplaced growths as a matter of routine.

Curtail rampant vigour, encourage flowering and fruiting by root pruning.

Where new roots grow over and cut into older ones, 'root grindling' occurs; the top root should be removed.

Remove dead or diseased wood.

Thin out overcrowded trees – especially those planted for instant effect.

Prop up branches of heavily laden tree fruits.

Examine supports and ties regularly – renew and adjust as necessary.

Knock snow off evergreens after heavy falls.

Tie in multi-stemmed conifers inconspicuously, immediately they show signs of spreading out of shape.

Hose down evergreens occasionally in towns to remove soot and grime.

Control weeds, pests and diseases.

Gather up prunings promptly.

Another form of height and spread reduction – pollarding – has earned a bad reputation: the familiar hat-stand effect of tortured forest trees in narrow streets is too well known to need description. But when correctly carried out on trees like young red- and yellow-barked willow, the result is quite pleasing. All year-old growth is cut back hard to well-budded knuckles or spurs in late March or April each year. Evergreens are *never* pollarded. And the pollarding of older trees is only a last resort to let in light while trees which will replace them are growing up alongside.

Lopping off heavy branches and tree felling are dangerous and best left to specialists. Similarly when it comes to bracing and tying in heavy limbs.

However, if dead, unsound or diseased wood needs to be cut back to sound, branches of up to about 8 cm (3 in) in diameter can generally be removed in safety. Splitting is the main hazard and can be avoided by cutting off a manageable portion at a time – always cutting about one third of the way through on the underside before cutting down vertically from above – a little further out from the trunk. Any redundant limb should be sawn off on the branch side of the collar between trunk and branch. Don't lop branches in frosty weather when splitting is hard to avoid.

Occasionally, soil levels near trees need to be adjusted. When lowering levels, cut away soil and roots but don't cut in closer to the trunk than a distance equal to half that from tree to branch tips. This work should be undertaken when the tree is dormant or when growth is at a low ebb. Build a retaining wall immediately to protect the rootball and prevent any washing down of the soil by rainfall.

When raising levels, clear any underplanting, then marry up with the surroundings by spreading coarse gravel over the entire root-run. If soil is used, there is a danger of root suffocation with any great depth of it.

Spur-pruning is normally reserved for highly intensive fruit production and for wall- and pergola-trained ornamentals. Spring-flowering trees and fruit crops of apple, pear and peach are summer pruned – ie they have new growths cut back to within three to five leaves of the main branch framework from June to August. Summer- and autumn-flowering wall-trained trees have new growths shortened back to within one or two buds of the main framework in late winter or spring.

Formation pruning and training is specialist work really best left to nurserymen. To give an idea of what is involved:

Free-standing trees In autumn, a year after initial training (see page 172), new growths arising from the topmost four shoots are shortened back by half to two-thirds. They form the primary branch framework. Continue to remove the feathers.

NOTE With some single-stemmed trees the feathers are an attraction – as with some birch, whitebeam and Lombardy Flowering Cherry. Planted as whips they are then left unpruned apart from trimming to shape.

Single-stem oblique cordons planted as whips have their side shoots cut back to one or two buds at planting. Annual summer pruning is then carried out in succeeding years. The central leader is cut out once the required height is reached – it may take up to six years.

Stump removal

Get rid of stumps after felling. If left they provide a source of infection for killer diseases like honey fungus (*Armillaria*).

Small stumps can often be eased out by digging round the base, cutting through the roots and then manhandling or winching the stump out. With large stumps, consider hiring a special chipper – preferably with an operator. After the stump has been exposed, it is decimated by the flails. Otherwise, there is little alternative but to saw the stumps off close to the ground and treat with chemical. Drill 2-cm ($\frac{1}{2}$-in) diameter holes into the butt and top of the stump. Make them 5-8 cm (2-3 in) deep and a similar distance apart and as near to the vertical as possible. Part-fill with potassium nitrate and plug with clay to prevent rain washing the chemicals away. Examine regularly and refill as necessary. It will take a stump anything from 2 to 10 years to rot away completely.

Your responsibilities

Needless worry and expense can be avoided if a few simple rules are followed:

Keep trees under control, both above and below ground. The owner is liable for any injury, damage or loss caused by his trees.

If a neighbour's trees encroach, roots and branches can be cut back only to the boundary.

Before cutting down trees of any significant size, establish the facts. For instance, in some countries it is an offence to fell – for example if a 'Tree Preservation Order' is in force or you are in a 'conservation area'.

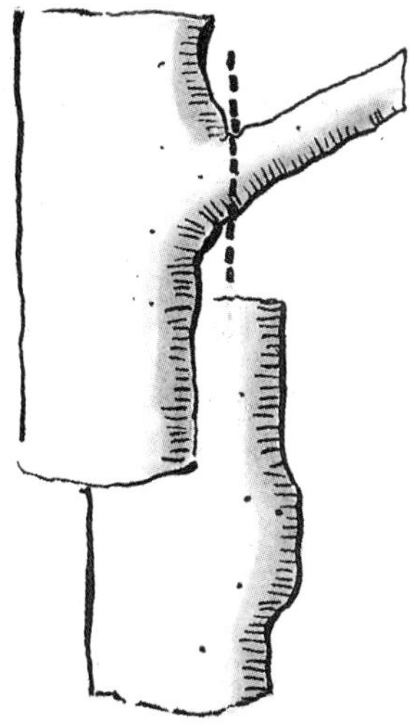

Pruning cuts

When removing dead or diseased branches from a tree, saw off the limb as neatly as possible on the branch side of the raised collar where the branch joins the main trunk. Leave the cut unpainted afterwards.

CONTAINER GROWING

It is best not to attempt to grow trees in containers unless you are prepared to devote time to them. They are completely dependent on regular feeding and watering; they also need occasional repotting and extra nursing throughout the year.

However, in many gardens, containers are the most practical – and sometimes the only – means of growing trees. Where, for instance, soil is unsuitable, infertile, too shallow, polluted or absent – as on the patio – trees can be grown. And in small gardens, containerizing trees restricts development while keeping the roots out of harm's way. Containers can be moved fairly easily – a useful attribute, too, when considering both display and plant care.

Choose tree containers carefully: they are likely to be occupied for a long time! Containers with a minimum depth and diameter of 38 cm (15 in) – up to 60 cm (2 ft) for established 3-m (10-ft) high trees – are about right. Look for stability – well-proportioned containers which are not top-heavy. For ease of potting and watering, the top should be as wide as or wider than the rest of the container. Durability and frost-resistance are of high priority, as is good drainage. Containers exposed to rain should have plenty of drainage holes in the base – not less than three 3-cm (1-in) holes per 38-cm (15-in) container. Check for reasonable insulation against frost and heat. Tree roots are very vulnerable in containers although special fibre liners will improve insulation.

Potting composts

Average garden soil is not suitable for containers, but proprietary potting composts overcome its failings. Soil-based mixtures contain sterilized loam plus peat, aggregate, lime and fertilizer. Peat-based mixtures are without loam, and other ingredients are adjusted accordingly. Soil-based mixtures are normally easier to manage, and they retain their physical properties longer than the peat-based ones. Being heavier, the containers are less likely to blow over. Peat-based mixtures are useful on roof gardens where excess weight must be avoided.

Potting composts are made up in differing strengths – weak, standard, strong or general-purpose – depending on the fertilizer content. Weak mixtures are normally reserved for slow-growing trees at their first potting. Standard composts are good subsequently for slow-growing varieties. Strong formulations are used for quick-growing and mature trees. General-purpose composts are popular, and fine for trees, provided fertilizer levels are boosted. Mix two cupfuls of bonemeal per bucketful of mix when potting large trees and top-dressing. Halve this quantity for small trees. Look for lime-free composts when potting acid-loving trees.

Preparing containers

Start with a clean, disinfected container. Soak new terracotta, concrete and simulated stone containers in water for at least a day before use. This washes away alkali and rehydrates the container so that it does not draw moisture out of the compost.

Move large, heavy containers into position – wherever possible near to a warm wall for winter protection – before filling and planting. Stand on a gravel bed so that drainage water can seep away easily. Watertight drip trays should only be used in summer, or when containers are raised on legs, otherwise you risk waterlogging the plant.

Cover the drainage holes with fine mesh netting or gauze to reduce loss of compost and to deter root-eating and other pests. Cover the base with clean crocks, small stones or gravel to a depth of an eighth of the height of the container.

Potting

The main rules on when to pot are given, right. Never move trees if the compost is frozen, dry or overwet. Autumn, after leaf fall, is a good time to pot lifted deciduous trees – provided reasonable winter protection is possible. In very cold districts leave potting until spring, which is a good time to move young container stock. Early spring is best for moving most container-grown trees.

Potting on and repotting

Part-fill the container, using sufficient moist compost to allow the tree to be set about 5 cm (2 in) below the rim. This allows for planting about 1 cm ($\frac{1}{2}$ in) deeper than before the move and

Moving trees in containers

There are several ways of taking the strain out of moving heavy pots of trees. Shown here are three practical methods. Get help if necessary to lift the pot, and always lift with your knees bent and your back straight, to avoid injury.

Place the tree on a plank and then insert several metal pipes at intervals under the plank and roll the plank over them, removing the end pipe and putting it at the front, and so on, as you move the plank.

When to repot trees

When trees are not thriving: with small, pale starved leaves.

When the compost dries out rapidly, even after frequent watering.

When thick roots grow out of the bottom of the container.

When the height or spread of the tree exceeds three times the diameter of the container.

leaves 3 cm (1 in) or so for watering. Next turn to the tree. Scrape off the top 2 cm ($\frac{3}{4}$ in) of old compost complete with weeds. Water and, while draining, prune out any diseased wood.

When moving a tree into a larger container, which should be at least 5 cm (2 in) wider than the original, hand-pick old crocks, lightly loosen up the sides of the rootball, and gently tease out the roots before spreading them out into the new container.

The accepted practice, once trees have reached the maximum size that is in keeping with their setting, is to repot into the same-sized container. This keeps a tree healthy without it getting appreciably larger. Carefully tease out as much of the old compost as possible. Then reduce rootball size by cutting away the main roots from the lower quarter of the rootball and taking in the width.

Position trees centrally and upright. Work fresh compost around the roots firming as filling proceeds. Peat-based mixtures must not be packed down too hard. But the new compost around the sides must be firmer than the rootball. Be sure to leave a space at the top for watering.

A split cane will suffice to support young trees. Many older trees don't need support.

Watering

Water immediately after potting – until it trickles out at the bottom. Use a can with fine rose to minimize washing away compost from around the roots. Subsequently water when the compost surface is almost dry – likely to be twice a day in hot weather. Always water before feeding, potting or top-dressing. Keep roots drier in winter – with containers protected from heavy downpours.

Mist over newly potted trees daily. When growing away nicely, spray after dry, hot or windy days.

Be wary about using self-watering pots. Many are fine in summer but difficult in winter.

Fertilizers

Actively growing trees, especially fruiting varieties, need fertilizers in spring and summer.

Root drenching with proprietary liquid fertilizer at monthly intervals, starting about three weeks after potting, gives good results. Dry fertilizer applications are an alternative – they are given less frequently – at six-week intervals – or as the makers direct.

It is not necessary to pot established trees every year. And in the years when potting is not carried out, it is sound practice to top-dress the trees. Scrape away the top 3 cm (1 in) or so of old compost – never try to dig it out or roots will be damaged. Top up with standard or strong potting compost and start liquid feeding two or three weeks afterwards.

General care

In summer, protect container trees from wind and hot sun with fine-mesh netting or screening.

In winter, in cold areas, insulate all containers with leaves, straw or sacking. Shelter all trees from wind, frost, snow and heavy rain. Move small trees under cover, providing they can be kept cool and have plenty of light and air. During severe weather, protect the roots and crowns of trees standing near walls with fine-mesh netting fixed to the wall and draped over the tree.

Special points for bonsai growing

☐ Spring is a good time to move bonsai.

☐ Buy hard-fired bonsai dishes. They withstand frost but are pricy.

☐ When potting bonsai from conventional pots to shallow dishes, take the rootball down by at least a third and thin the crown to compensate. Always use bonsai compost: two parts standard soil-based potting compost to one each of sphagnum peat and coarse sand.

☐ When repotting, tease out as much of the old compost as possible before root pruning. After positioning many bonsai must be wired into place.

☐ Newly potted bonsai must be misted over every day. Bonsai should always be watered from below by standing in shallow water.

☐ Top up bonsai compost every six weeks or so – whenever roots are exposed.

☐ It is vital to shade bonsai from strong sun. And overwinter them under frames protected from severe weather and sheltered from wind.

Insert a large, heavy-duty piece of sacking under the pot and pull the sacking along.

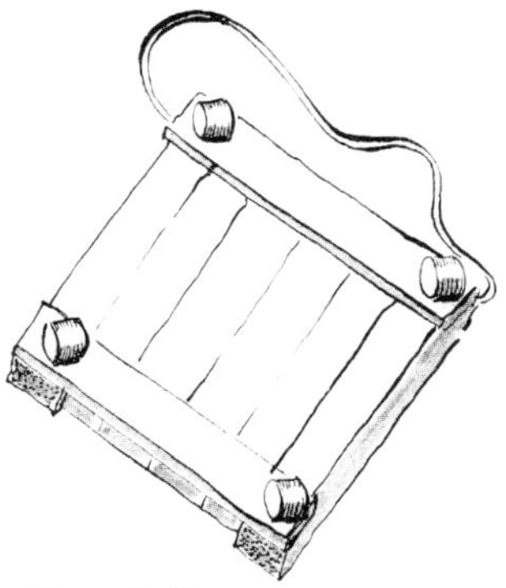

Best of all, construct a simple stout platform of 4-5 planks nailed to two supporting struts, with a caster at each corner of the base.

Pests & Diseases

A HEALTHY TREE will resist disease and stand a good chance of shaking off most pest attacks. This underlines the importance of choosing trees to suit the garden, sound cultivation and timely attention to detail.

In the average garden, it is usual to wait until the first signs of trouble appear and then take appropriate action. The alternative is to adopt a routine preventive spray programme. Basically the idea is to anticipate problems and apply chemicals or take other remedial steps, before trouble strikes but under normal circumstances such a widespread use of chemicals is not a good idea and environmentally inappropriate.

Correct diagnosis is not always easy. The important thing, before starting treatment, is to establish whether the problem is caused by a disorder, a pest or disease. Always use approved chemicals and follow instructions carefully.

Choice of treatment

Spraying with proprietary chemicals in liquid form is popular and effective. Never spray in strong sun, during frost, just before rain or on windy days.

Soil drench when disinfecting suspect ground prior to planting. And when cleaning up after removing a diseased tree. Break the soil down finely beforehand.

Fumigant powders/granules, worked into the soil, take care of many soil pests. Again useful when planting on suspect land.

Aerosol sprays are convenient for small scale spot treatment on young trees and bonsai.

Traps and baits are useful when growing fruit. For example greasebands wrapped round the trunks of apple and pear trees in September will trap winter moths as they make their way up into the tree to lay their eggs. And corrugated card tied round branches in June will trap grubs of the codling moth – the cause of maggoty apples.

Biological controls are beginning to offer a wide range of environmentally safe pest controls for garden trees. Watch for developments.

Disorders

Among the problems most likely to affect trees are non-infectious disorders. These are brought on by: poor growing conditions; adverse weather; faulty nutrition, watering or pruning; or the misapplication of weedkillers, pesticides and fungicides. For instance, the exudation of yellow gum onto bark and buds of cherry and plum inevitably follows if severely pruned in late winter. Similarly, birch, maple and walnut are likely to lose an excessive amount of sap through pruning cuts. These trees are all best pruned in autumn – never after the sap has begun to rise in late winter.

Browning/dying foliage The common causes are scorch from strong sun, wind or frost and root damage owing to injury, waterlogging or intolerable dryness.

Keep all newly planted trees well watered – and spray over the foliage – vital during hot, dry, windy weather. Use anti-wilt sprays on newly planted conifers. Temporary shading helps.

Bud, flower and fruitlet drop The common causes are natural shed following overproduction and root injury or dryness typical of shallow soils.

Keep roots moist and mulch generously.

Failure to set fruit This is usually caused by frost, storms, cold winds or lack of a nearby pollinating variety.

Net early flowering wall fruits for frost protection and shelter them from cold winds. Plant pollinator varieties. Self-pollinating and family trees are notable exceptions.

Chlorosis (leaf yellowing) This is often caused by attempting to grow acid-loving trees in limy soil, or watering with hard mains water.

To avoid it, grow acid-lovers in containers of lime-free compost if the soil is chalky or overlies limestone. Use rainwater for watering container trees in hard-water areas. The recognized method of control of chlorosis is to drench with iron sequestrene. However, this is expensive and uneconomical for all but the smallest trees.

Diseases

Diseases can spread from tree to tree.

Fungal diseases – moulds, mildews, rusts and scabs – are amongst the easiest to diagnose since they have characteristic outgrowths. For instance, trunk rots and honey fungus produce mushroom-like fungi. Fungal diseases are usually spread by spores and are prevented with fungicides.

Bacterial diseases cause rotting and wilting. Some are incurable, others are controlled with bactericides. Like fungal diseases they are spread by wind and water – but to a greater extent by contact with infected tissue, tools and hands. Fire blight is especially bad, attacking mainly the *Rosaceae* family. Foliage, flowers, shoots – even whole branches – seem scorched by fire. Then they wither, blacken and die. Trees most at risk are apple, pear, crab, cotoneaster, thorn and whitebeam. Cut back withered wood well into sound wood and disinfect pruning tools between cuts. In areas where fire blight is prevalent opt for non-susceptible varieties when replanting.

Virus diseases are most likely to become a problem for intensive fruit growers. Stunted trees carrying deformed, twisted, mottled or discoloured leaves and flowers are typical. There is no practical cure. Virus diseases are carried in the sap, spread on hands and tools and by sap sucking insects like aphids.

Cankers Canker-causing organisms usually gain entry through pruning wounds and stubs, insect injury or diseased tissue. Trees most at risk are apple, peach, plum, cherry, poplar and ash. Keep plant as stress-free as possible with regular watering and feeding.

A typical canker forms a circular/oval patch and is surrounded by raised roughened bark with a sunken, sometimes rotting centre.

Remove cankers promptly. With small cankers, cut out the affected area completely and smooth over with a sharp knife. Where a branch is completely encircled with cankers, it is best to remove the branch.

Honey fungus If victim to honey fungus, the tree wilts progressively and dies. Honey-coloured toadstools appear at or near ground level. The disease spreads mainly by blackish-brown bootlace-like strands travelling out from the tree underground, but also by windborne spores. Almost all trees are at risk.

Dig out diseased trees along with bootlace strands. Drench the ground with proprietary honey fungus fungicide to contain the spread.

Mildews These appear as whitish meal-like dusts on leaves, shoot tips, buds and flowers. They weaken and disfigure the tree although some varieties tolerate repeated infections with little long-term damage.

Cut out badly affected shoots. Apply fungicide at the first signs, and repeat throughout the growing season. Do not spray edible crops once the fruits have started to ripen.

Peach leaf curl This attacks almond, peach and nectarine trees. Puckered, deformed leaves first take on a reddish hue – later becoming white. Premature leaf fall is typical. Trees are weakened. Where there is a history of the disease, spray with a fungicide in spring and autumn.

Silver leaf A characteristic silvering of leaves is followed by purplish fungal outgrowths on dead/dying branches. Cut back all branches carrying dead shoots and silvered foliage until the wood is completely free from brown staining.

Pests

Pests come in a variety and betray themselves by remaining near the scene of their activities.

Aphids Colonies congregate around growing points and undersides of leaves which become distorted, twisted and puckered.

Spray with insecticide at first signs. Following severe attacks on fruit trees use tar oil winter wash to destroy overwintering eggs.

Birds Ripening fruits are pecked and spoilt. Net over wall fruits.

Caterpillars When leaves, buds, flowers, shoots and fruits are eaten and holed, caterpillars will often be found close by. Handpick the caterpillars in the case of small-scale attacks on young trees. Otherwise spray with insecticide during the growing season and follow up with tar oil winter wash – deciduous trees only.

Red spider mites Look for mottled and yellowing leaves with massed red or yellowish minute insects on the undersides. In bad attacks spider-like webbing is visible. Leaf bronzing, premature defoliation and stunted growth are likely. In the main it is young trees and fruit trees which suffer the most.

During prolonged hot weather hose young trees with water to discourage the mite. Spray with miticide at the first signs of attack – or where there is a history of trouble. But do not spray fruit trees as crops are ripening.

INDEX

Page numbers in *italic* refer to the illustrations; **bold** page numbers refer to entries in the Guide to Garden Trees.

Index compiled by Hilary Bird

LISTS OF TREES

A selection of some of the best trees for specific purposes or effects is given on these pages. More detailed information on the species can be found in the Guide to Garden Trees on pp 100-165.

S = up to 8 m (25 ft)
M = 8-20 m (25-65 ft)
L = over 20 m (65 ft)

Spring flowering
(March/April)
Acer rubrum L
Amelanchier laevis S
A. lamarckii
Azara integrifolia S
Camellia japonica and cvs S
C. reticulata and cvs
C. sasanqua and cvs
C. × *williamsii* and cvs
Cercis canadensis M
C. siliquastrum
Cornus florida and cvs M
Cydonia oblonga M
Drimys winteri M
Magnolia (many) S-M
Malus (many) M
Prunus (many) M
Pyrus communis M
Rhododendron (many) S-M
Salix caprea (catkins) S-M
Sophora tetraptera M

Summer flowering
(May-August)
Abies koreana (cones) M
Aesculus (all) L
Buddleia alternifolia M
B. davidii
Callistemon citrinus M
Catalpa (all) M
Ceanothus (all) S-M
Clethra arborea M
Cornus capitata S-M
C. kousa
C. nuttallii
Crataegus (many species) M
Cytisus battandieri S
Davidia involucrata M-L
Embothrium coccineum M
Eucryphia glutinosa S-M
E. × *nymansensis*
Genista aetnensis S-M
Halesia carolina M
H. monticola
Hibiscus syriacus S
Hoheria glabrata M
H. sexstylosa
Koelreuteria paniculata M
Laburnum (all) M
Lagerstroemia indica S-M
Leptospermum scoparium S
Ligustrum lucidum M
Liriodendron tulipifera L
Magnolia grandiflora M
M. sinensis S
M. wilsonii S
Mespilus germanica S-M
Metrosideros robusta M
Oxydendrum arboreum M
Paulownia fargesii M
P. tomentosa
Rhododendron (many) S-M
Robinia pseudacacia L
R. hispida M
Stewartia pseudocamellia M
Styrax japonica M
S. obassia
Syringa oblata S
S. reflexa
S. vulgaris

Autumn colour
Acer – many species but especially
A. cappadocicum L
A. circinatum M
A. griseum M
A. japonicum and cvs S-M
A. palmatum and cvs S-M
A. rubrum L
Aesculus flava L
Carya (all) L
Cercidiphyllum japonicum M-L
Cercis canadensis M
Cladrastis lutea M
Cornus alba S
C. florida and cvs M
Cotinus coggygria S
C. obovatus M
Crataegus crus-galli M
C. phaenopyrum
C. × *prunifolia*
Cydonia oblonga M
Euonymus europaeus S-M
E. oxyphyllus
Fothergilla major S
Franklinia alatamaha M
Ginkgo biloba L
Koelreuteria paniculata M
Larix (all) L
Liquidambar styraciflua L
Liriodendron chinense L
L. tulipifera
Mespilus germanica S-M
Metasequoia glyptostroboides L
Nothofagus procera L
Nyssa sylvatica L
Oxydendrum arboreum M
Parrotia persica M
Populus tremula M
Prunus sargentii M
Pseudolarix amabilis M-L
Pyrus calleryana 'Chanticleer' M
Quercus palustris L
Q. rubra
Rhus typhina M
Stewartia pseudocamellia M
Sorbus 'Embley' M
S. 'Joseph Rock'
S. vilmorinii
Taxodium ascendens M-L
T. distichum
Zelkova serrata L

Winter interest
Acer palmatum 'Senkaki' (shoot colouration) S-M
Arbutus × *andrachnoides* (bark colour) S
Betula (most – bark colour) – especially
B. albo-sinensis M
B. nigra
Cornus alba (stem colour) S
C. mas (flowers) M
Corylus avellana 'Contorta' (general habit) S
Cotoneaster (most – berries) S-M
Elaeagnus angustifolia (berries) M
Eucalyptus (many – bark colour) M-L
Fraxinus excelsior 'Jaspidea' (shoot colouration) L
Garrya elliptica (catkins) S
Hamamelis (flowers) S
Ilex (most – berries) S-M
Malus (most – fruit) – especially
M. 'Golden Hornet'
M. 'John Downie'
Myrtus luma (bark colour) M
Rhododendron hodgsonii (and many other species) – bark colour and leaf form S-M
Salix alba 'Chermisina' M
S. daphnoides (shoot colour)
S. matsudana 'Tortuosa'
Sorbus (most – berries) M
Sycopsis sinensis S
Viburnum × *bodnantense* (flowers) S

Evergreens
Abies (all) L
Acacia dealbata M
Araucaria araucana L
Arbutus (all) M
Azara integrifolia S
Buxus sempervirens S
Callistemon citrinus M
Camellia (all) S
Ceanothus arboreus S-M
C. thyrsiflorus
Cedrus (all) L
Chamaecyparis (all) L
Chamaerops humilis M
Citrus (all) S
Clethra arborea M
Coffea arabica S
Cordyline australis S
Cornus capitata M
Cotoneaster (many) S-M
Cryptomeria japonica L
Cunninghamia lanceolata M
Cupressus (all) L
Drimys winteri M
Embothrium coccineum (some forms) M
Erica arborea S
Eriobotrya japonica S-M
Eucalyptus (all) M-L
Euonymus japonicus S
Fatsia japonica S
Fortunella margarita S
Garrya elliptica S
Griselinia littoralis M
Hebe salicifolia S
Hoheria sexstylosa M
Ilex (most – not *I. verticillata*) M
Jacaranda acutifolia M
Juniperus (all) S-M
Laurus nobilis M
Ligustrum lucidum S-M
L. ovalifolium★
Magnolia grandiflora M
Metrosideros robusta M
Myrtus luma M
Olea europaea S-M
Phillyrea latifolia M
Photinia serrulata M
Picea (all) L
Pinus (all) L
Pittosporum (all) M
Quercus × *hispanica*★ L
Q. ilex
Rhododendron (most) M
Schefflera actinophylla S
Sciadopitys verticillata M
Sequoia sempervirens L

Sequoiadendron giganteum L
Sophora tetraptera M
Stranvaesia davidiana M
Sycopsis sinensis S
Taxus (all) M
Thuja (all) L
Trachycarpus fortunei M
Trochodendron aralioides M
Tsuga (all) L
Viburnum (some) S–M

*Deciduous in hard winters

Suitable for providing shelter

Acer campestre M
A. platanoides L
A. pseudoplatanus L
Alnus cordata M–L
A. incana
Betula pendula M
B. pubescens
Chamaecyparis lawsoniana L
Crataegus monogyna M
Cryptomeria japonica L
Cupressus macrocarpa L
Fraxinus excelsior L
Picea omorika L
Pinus nigra L
P. sylvestris
Populus alba L
P. tremula M
Quercus robur L
Sorbus aria M
S. aucuparia

Tolerant of clipping

Buxus sempervirens S
Carpinus betulus M
Chamaecyparis lawsoniana L
Cotoneaster salicifolius M
Crataegus monogyna M
× *Cupressocyparis leylandii* L
Cupressus macrocarpa L
Griselinia littoralis M
Ilex × *altaclarensis* and cvs* M
I. aquifolium and cvs*
Laurus nobilis S–M
Ligustrum ovalifolium S
Quercus ilex L
Rhododendron ponticum S–M
*Taxus baccata** M
Thuja plicata L
Tsuga canadensis L
T. heterophylla

*Particularly suitable for topiary

Suitable for dry soils

Acer negundo M
Acacia dealbata M
Ailanthus altissima L
Callistemon citrinus M
Caragana arborescens S
Castanea dentata L
Cedrus (all) L
Cotoneaster (many) S–M
Cupressus arizonica L
C. sempervirens
Elaeagnus angustifolia M
Erica arborea S
Genista aetnensis M
Gleditsia (all) L
Jacaranda acutifolia M
Juniperus (all) S–M
Populus tremula M
P. alba L
Platanus (all) L
Pinus (all) L
Pittosporum tobira S
Robinia (all) L
Tamarix (all) S

Suitable for wet conditions

Alnus (all) M–L
Amelanchier (all) S–M
Betula nigra M
B. papyrifera
B. pendula
B. pubescens
Cornus alba S
Crataegus oxyacantha M
Ilex verticillata S
Mespilus germanica M
Metasequoia glyptostroboides L
Populus (most) L
Pyrus communis M
Quercus palustris L
Salix (all) M–L
Sambucus (all) M
Sorbus aucuparia M
Taxodium ascendens L
T. distichum
Viburnum opulus S

Tolerant of calcareous soils

Acer campestre M
A. negundo M
A. platanoides L
A. pseudoplatanus L
Aesculus (most) L
Buddleia davidii M
Buxus sempervirens S
Carpinus betulus M
Ceanothus (all) S–M
Cercis siliquastrum M
Cotoneaster (all) S–M
Crataegus oxyacantha M
Elaeagnus angustifolia M
Fagus sylvatica L
Fraxinus excelsior L
F. ornus
Hebe (all) S
Laurus nobilis M
Ligustrum (all) S–M
Malus (most) M
Morus nigra M
Phillyrea latifolia M
Photinia serrulata M
Populus alba L
Prunus (Sato cherries) M
Sambucus (all) M
Sorbus aria M
Syringa (all) S
Taxus baccata M
Thuja occidentalis L
T. plicata
Ulmus (most) L

Coloured or variegated foliage

Acer palmatum cvs (y and p) S–M
A. japonicum cvs (y and p) S–M
A. platanoides 'Drummondii' (v) L
A. pseudoplatanus 'Brilliantissimum' (y)
A.p. 'Worleei' (y)
Alnus glutinosa 'Aurea' (y) M–L
A. incana 'Aurea' (y)
Aralia elata 'Aureomarginata' (v) S
A.e. 'Variegata' (v)
Betula pendula Purpurea' (p) M
Castanea sativa 'Aureomarginata' (v) L
Catalpa bignonioides 'Aurea' M
C. × *erubescens* 'Purpurea'
Cedrus altantica 'Glauca' (bluish) L
Cornus alba 'Elegantissima' (v) S
C.a. 'Spaethii' (v) S
C. alternifolia 'Argentea' (v) M
C. controversa 'Variegata' (v) M
C. mas 'Aurea' (y) M
C.m. 'Elegantissima' (v) M
Cotinus coggygria 'Royal Purple' (p) S
Euonymous japonicus 'Ovatus Aureus' (y) S
Gleditsia triacanthos 'Sunburst' (y) L
Ilex × *altaclarensis* cvs (y and v) M
I. aquifolium cvs (y and v)
Juniperus chinensis 'Aurea' (y) M
Laurus nobilis 'Aurea' (y) S–M
Ligustrum lucidum 'Tricolor' (v) S–M
L. ovalifolium 'Aureum' (y)
Liquidambar styraciflua 'Aurea' (y) L
Liriodendron tulipifera 'Aureomarginata' (v) L
Pinus sylvestris 'Aurea' (y) L
Populus 'Serotina Aurea' L
P. × *candicans* 'Aurea' (v)
Quercus robur 'Atropurpurea' (p) L
Q.r. 'Concordia' (y)
Q.r. 'Variegata' (v)
Robinia pseudacacia 'Frisia' (v) L
Sambucus nigra 'Aurea' M
S. racemosa 'Plumosa Aurea' (y)

v = variegated
y = yellow/golden
p = purple

Pollution tolerant

Acer platanoides L
A. pseudoplatanus L
Aesculus hippocastanum L
Alnus cordata M–L
A. glutinosa
A. incana
Amelanchier (all) S–M
Aralia elata S
Araucaria araucana L
Betula papyrifera M
B. pendula
B. pubescens
Buddleia davidii M
Buxus sempervirens S
Camellia japonica and cvs S
C. × *williamsii* and cvs
Carpinus betulus M
Catalpa bignonioides M
Cedrus (all) L
Chamaecyparis lawsoniana L
Cornus alba S
Cotoneaster (most) S–M
Crataegus (most) M
× *Cupressocyparis leylandii* L
Davidia involucrata M–L
Euonymus japonicus S
Fatsia japonica S
Fraxinus excelsior L
Garrya elliptica S
Ginkgo biloba L

Pollution tolerant (ctd)
Ilex × *altaclarensis* M
I. aquifolium
Laburnum (all) M
Ligustrum ovalifolium S
Liriodendron tulipifera L
Magnolia cordata M
M. × *loebneri* M
M. × *soulangiana* M
Malus (most) M
Mespilus germanica M
Metasequoia glyptostroboides L
Morus nigra M
Phillyrea latifolia M
Picea omorika L
Pinus nigra L
Platanus (all) L
Populus (most) L
Prunus (many species and cvs) M
Quercus × *hispanica* L
Q. ilex
Robinia pseudacacia L
Rhus typhina S
Salix (most) M-L
Sambucus nigra M
Sorbus aria M
S. aucuparia
Ulmus (most) L
Viburnum (most)

Suitable for containers
(Many species can be pot grown whilst young but quickly deteriorate)
Buxus sempervirens S
Callistemon citrinus M
Camellia (all) S
Citrus (most) S
Coffea arabica S
Ficus carica S
Ilex × *altaclarensis* and cvs M
I. aquifolium and cvs
Laurus nobilis M
Magnolia stellata S
Rhododendron (many) S-M

Edible fruit
Carya glabra L
C. ovata
Castanea sativa L
Citrus (all) S
Corylus avellana S
Cydonia oblonga S
Diospyros kaki M
D. virginiana
Eriobotrya japonica S-M
Ficus carica S
Fortunella margarita S
*Ginkgo biloba** L
Juglans (most) L
Malus (most) M
Mespilus germanica M
Morus nigra M
M. alba
Olea europaea S-M
*Pinus pinea** M
Poncirus trifoliata S
Prunus armeniaca M
*P. cerasus**
P. dulcis
P. persica
*P. spinosa**
Pyrus communis M
*Sambucus nigra** M
*Sorbus aucuparia** M

*Rarely eaten raw or without some preparation.

Hardiness zones
The chart shows the average minimum winter temperatures for each zone. A tree labelled Zone 5, for example, in the *Guide to Garden Trees* is unlikely to withstand regions with colder winters than the temperatures given for this zone in the chart.

Zone	Centigrade	Fahrenheit
1	below −46°	below −50°
2	−46° to −40°	−50° to −40°
3	−40° to −34°	−40° to −30°
4	−34° to −28°	−30° to −20°
5	−28° to −22°	−20° to −10°
6	−22° to −16°	−10° to −0°
7	−16° to −12°	0° to 10°
8	−12° to −6°	10° to 20°
9	−6° to −1°	20° to 30°
10	−1° to −4°	30° to 40°

Author's acknowledgments
David Palliser for all his help with writing the book; Leo Pemberton and David Carr for their expertise; Arthur Hellyer for writing the foreword; David Cresswell and 'The Men of the Trees'.

Penny David and Joanna Chisholm for their editorial help; Paul Meyer for information for the American edition and Mark Flanagan for providing the lists of useful trees.

Photographs
Brian Carter/GPL 53L, 56BR, 61BL, 105BL, 107R, 115R, 145B, 146B
Eric Crichton 41, 99, 114L, 135R, 148BL
Henk Dijkman/GPL 21, 30, 40, 48 (main pic), 51 (inset top), 70, 75, 79, 92, 102 (inset left), 111, 150T
Penelope Doan 161
Inge Espen-Hansen 87, 116T, 158T, 162B
Robert Estall 126L
Derek Fell 53R, 82, 112/3R, 115L
Philippe Ferret 86L, 121, 122L, 122TR, 129, 130
Vaughan Fleming/GPL 52, 58, 61BR, 133T
John Glover/GPL 125T, 125BR
Marijke Heuff 36, 39, 46/7C, 49, 71R, 78, 83, 94, 105T, 119T, 138/9R, 148/9T
Neil Holmes 125BL, 141, 149BR, 156T
Lamontagne 151B, 154T
Georges Lévêque 2, 31, 33, 34L, 35, 50, 93, 108, 134/5C, 142/3L, 153R, 160T
Tania Midgley 116B, 117
Hugh Palmer 16, 57, 66
Joanne Pavia 1
Perderau-Thomas/GPL 20, 22, 27, 34C, 38, 55 (Apremont), 56T, 65, 69, 73, 74, 77, 85R, 90, 95, 96, 98R, 106/7 (main pic), 109, 112L, 119B, 127, 131, 132, 133B, 145T, 146T, 152/3L, 159C, 159B, 163T
Gary Rogers/GPL 7, 47R, 61TL, 62, 64, 106L, 123
David Russell/GPL 54, 104, 107 (inset), 138L, 144, 155, 159T
Wolfram Stehling 128
Ron Sutherland/GPL 18, 19, 23, 80, 84L, 84/5C, 88, 89, 91, 124, 140, 154B, 157, 160B
Don Wildridge 59, 61TR, 120T, 126C, 143R
Cynthia Woodyard/GPL 71L, 122B, 151T
Steven Wooster/GPL 9, 24, 25, 26, 28, 29, 32, 43, 45, 46L, 48 (inset), 51 (main pic & inset right), 56BL, 60, 68, 76, 81R, 97, 98L, 100, 102/3 (main pic & inset right), 105BR, 110, 118, 120B, 134L, 136, 137, 147, 150B, 156B, 158B, 162T, 163B, 164

R = right, L = left, T = top, B = bottom, C = centre
GPL = Garden Picture Library (01-585 0277).

Illustrations
Madeleine David 10/11, 166-181
Shirley Felts (The Garden Studio) 13, 14/15